An introduction
to the Laws of the
Duchy of Cornwall,
the Isles of Scilly,
and Devon

Other books in Cornish and about Cornwall from Evertype

Gooth ha Gouvreus (Jane Austen, tr. Nicholas Williams 2014)

Tredden in Scath (Jerome K. Jerome, tr. Nicholas Williams 2014)

Towards a Cornish Philosophy (Alan Kent 2013)

An Gwyns i'n Helyk (Kenneth Graham, tr. Nicholas Williams 2013)

Gwerryans an Planettys (H. G. Wells, tr. Nicholas Williams 2013)

Ky Teylu Baskerville (Arthur Conan Doyle, tr. Nicholas Williams 2012)

Flehes an Hens Horn (Edith Nesbit, tr. Nicholas Williams 2012)

Phyllis in Piskie-land (J. Henry Harris 2012)

An Beybel Sans: The Holy Bible in Cornish (tr. Nicholas Williams 2011)

Whedhlow ha Drollys a Gernow Goth (Nigel Roberts, tr. Nicholas Williams 2011)

The Beast of Bodmin Moor: Best Goon Brèn (Alan Kent, tr. Neil Kennedy 2011)

Enys Tresour (Robert Louis Stevenson, tr. Nicholas Williams 2010)

Whedhlow Kernowek: Stories in Cornish (A.S.D. Smith, ed. Nicholas Williams 2010)

Henry Jenner's Handbook of the Cornish Language (ed. Michael Everson 2010)

The Cult of Relics: Devocyon dhe Greryow (Alan Kent, tr. Nicholas Williams, 2010)

Jowal Lethesow: Whedhel a'm West a Gernow (Craig Weatherhill, tr. Nicholas Williams, 2009)

Skeul an Tavas: A coursebook in Standard Cornish (Ray Chubb, 2009)

Kensa Lyver Redya (Harriette Treadwell & Margaret Free, tr. Eddie Foirbeis Climo, 2009)

Adro dhe'n Bÿs in Peswar Ugans Dëdh (Jules Verne, abridged and tr. Kaspar Hocking, 2009)

A Concise Dictionary of Cornish Place-Names (Craig Weatherhill, 2009)

Alys in Pow an Anethow (Lewis Carroll, tr. Nicholas Williams, 2009)

Form and Content in Revived Cornish (Michael Everson, Craig Weatherhill, Ray Chubb, Bernard Deacon, Nicholas Williams, 2006)

Towards Authentic Cornish (Nicholas Williams, 2006)

Writings on Revived Cornish (Nicholas Williams, 2006)

Cornish Today (Nicholas Williams, 2006)

An introduction
to the Laws of the
Duchy of Cornwall,
the Isles of Scilly,
and Devon

John Kirkhope

evertype

2014

Published by Evertype, Cnoc Sceichín, Leac an Anfa, Cathair na Mart, Co. Mhaigh Eo, Éire. *www.evertype.com.*

First edition 2014.

A catalogue record for this book is available from the British Library.

ISBN-10 1-78201-072-6
ISBN-13 978-1-78201-072-2

Typeset in Baskerville by Michael Everson.

Cover design by Michael Everson.

Printed and bound by LightningSource.

Contents

For my beautiful long-suffering

and patient wife

Lisa

Foreword

Cornwall is different. In what other part of England do you see the County,[1] Town and street names written in two languages? In how many English Counties do you find a movement campaigning for its own Assembly? There is pride in the Black and White Flag of St Piran which is displayed everywhere in preference to the flag of St George or the Union Flag. Cornwall's story, so long neglected, is now studied in its own right and not simply as an adjunct to the history of England. The people of Cornwall over the centuries have fought and died to have their individual status and character recognized.[2] That distinctiveness is now being recognized and one of the ways in which Cornwall is singular is its unique legal heritage and this deserves to be even more widely known. This has now been recognized by Government since the Cornish will now be recognized under the European Framework Convention for the Protection of National Minorities as a National Minority.

Although the focus of this work is the Laws of the Duchy of Cornwall (by which in this context I mean the geographic place

---

1 I am aware that for some to describe Cornwall as a County of England is highly controversial.

2 For those interested in pursuing this further I would recommend Stoyle, M., *West Britons—Cornish Identities and the Early British State* (2002), Stoyle, M. "Pagans of Paragons? Images of the Cornish during the English Civil War" (1996) *English Historical review* Volume 111 No 441 pp 299-323 and Stoyle, M., "The Dissidence of Despair: Rebellion and Identity in Early Modern Cornwall" (1999) *Journal of British Studies* Volume 38 No 4 pp 423-444

called Cornwall) I have devoted a Chapter to some of the laws of Devon, including a consideration of Stannary Law in so far as it applies to that County. There is also discussion at various points on legal issues specific to the Isles of Scilly.

I am a lawyer, not a historian although I have a passion for history, and as a lawyer those laws which are particular to Cornwall and, to a lesser extent, Devon and are still applicable in the 21st Century are of special interest to me. It is worthy of emphasis that certain ancient laws and customs, in particular Stannary Law, although not as relevant today, are still part of the law of England and Wales. They continue to give rights which are capable of being exercised.

This is not meant to be legal textbook, which would be very dull, it is intended as a brief introduction to a fascinating topic. The Bibliography provides details of other material for those who want to develop their interest further.

One could not examine the Laws of the Duchy of Cornwall, Devon or the Isles of Scilly without at some point considering the Duchy of Cornwall (by which I mean the Duchy in its broader sense). For those interested in a detailed examination of the origin, evolution and contemporary legal status of the Duke and Duchy of Cornwall I would refer readers to my thesis.[3]

I would be delighted to hear from those who may wish to discuss, challenge or supplement any of the material contained in this booklet and may be contacted at john.kirkhope@gmail.com.

John Kirkhope
Perranporth, 2014

---

3   Kirkhope, J., *The Duchy of Cornwall—A Feudal Remnant* (2013) Thesis (Ph.D.) University of Plymouth

Chapter 1

The Stannaries

The Stannary system "might almost be termed territorial independence..."[4]

Introduction

There is much misunderstanding with regard to the Stannaries which needs to be untangled but before doing so a brief background will provide context.

Miners and Mining and the Law

Mining is a dangerous and difficult business presenting complex problems for the lawyer. It is not surprising that special laws and customs developed not simply in the United Kingdom but throughout Europe and beyond to deal with the issues which arose. To take a simple example, you might sink a shaft in your land which then passes under the property of your neighbour and maybe under the foreshore: the question which immediately arises is what rights do your neighbours have to the minerals lying under their land which you are mining? What if a miner diverts a stream or river to wash the ore which is being extracted and in so doing everyone living downstream is deprived of their water source?[5]

The structure which developed within Cornwall and Devon was called the Stannaries, which included an administration

---

4 Rowe, J., *Cornwall in the Age of the Industrial Revolution* (1953) (2nd Edition St Austell 1993) p 195

5 For more on this see Sir Edward Smirke *Case of Vice against Thomas with an Appendix of Records and Documents on the Early History of Tin Mines in Cornwall* (1843)

and legal system, law court, "Parliaments" and a form of taxation called "coinage".[6] The Stannaries of Cornwall were initially concerned with tin mining but eventually covered "all metal mining".[7] The word "Stannary" is derived from the Latin *Stannum* meaning tin. Devon's Stannaries were similar to but differed in detail from those of Cornwall. The Duchy of Cornwall, via an official, who is still appointed, called the Lord Warden of the Stannaries, was responsible for the Stannaries in both Devon and Cornwall.

Miners within the Stannaries had liberties by which their position was guaranteed. It is said:

> "(he) formed with his fellows of the district a state within a state. He paid taxes not as an Englishman but as a miner. His law was not the law of the realm but the law of the mine. He obeyed the King only when his orders were communicated through the Warden of the mines, and even then so long only as he (the Warden) respected mining law. His courts were the mine courts, his parliament the mine parliament. He owed no lord, lived no manor, paid no dues, and was subject to no feudal levy and might be called out by the King only under important restriction."[8]

Stannary Law related not only to mining and associated matters but covered all aspects of the lives of those who were engaged in tin affairs. The Stannary Courts heard cases whether related to tin mining or not and whether the other

---

and G. R. Lewis *The Stannaries—A Study of the Medieval Tin Miners of Cornwall and Devon* (1908)

6   The name "coinage" arose from the process of assaying. A *coign* was clipped from each block of tin to test in order to fix the price. (Midlgley, L Margaret, *Ministers' Accounts of the Earldom of Cornwall 1296-1297* (1942) p xxvii)

7   Stannaries Act 1836

8   Page, W., *The Victoria History of the Counties of England and Wales* (1906) p 523

party was a miner or not. Indeed "privileged tinners", by the Charters of 1201 and 1305 (See Appendix I), were not to be hauled before ordinary Courts unless the case concerned murder, manslaughter and mayhem. Cases in which one of the parties was a "foreigner" or "non tinner" were held before juries consisting half tinners and half "non tinners". The Lord Warden of the Stannaries mustered the men of the Stannaries for service in times of danger.[9] The Stannaries had their own regiment until 1913.[10] A curious echo of this provision can be found in the Reserve Forces Act 1996 which provides that if an Association is formed in Devon and Cornwall under the provisions of that Act then the Lord Warden of the Stannaries shall be ex-officio member.[11]

Dr John Rowe stated the Stannary system "might almost be termed territorial semi-independence."[12] According to Lewis:

> "the Stannaries were a peculiar jurisdiction under the operation of certain laws… for the administration of which a royal officer was responsible…. The head of the Stannary system was the Duke of Cornwall."[13]

It should be emphasized that the Stannaries of Cornwall and Devon represented a very considerable source of income, influence and power for the Duke and Duchy of Cornwall.

---

9   See, for example file at Cornwall Record Office X355/48 "Precept from Lord Warden of the Stannaries to Richard Hawke, chief constable, to issue warrants to petty constables of all parishes in his hundred, to return list of all miners aged between 18 and 45 liable to serve in Miners' Regiment of Militia."

10 Cornish Mining World Heritage: http://www.cornish-mining.org.uk/story/medieval.htm

11 Reserve Forces Act 1996 Schedule 4 section 7

12 Rowe, J., *Cornwall in the Age of the Industrial Revolution* (1953) (2nd Edition 1993) p 195

13 Lewis, G R., *The Stannaries: A Study of the Medieval Tin Miners of Cornwall and Devon* (1908) p 108

The Origins of Stannary Law

Sir George Harrison said the Stannaries of Cornwall and Devon "was in existence at a period infinitely more remote than the reign of Richard I."[14] He went on to say:

> "Their coexistence throughout all periods of still existing record is undoubted; and this consideration might probably carry the Stannary Jurisdiction very nearly to the time of the Phoenician traffic with Britain for Tin."

Lord Coke stated in the early seventeenth century:

> "This jurisdiction is guided by special laws, by customs and by prescription, time out of mind."[15]

Stannary law, to quote Professor Robert Pennington from his comprehensive examination of the subject:

> "is still formally a part of the law of England. It is moreover one of the oldest parts of the law, for its origins predates the Norman Conquest, possibly even the Anglo Saxons…"[16]

The Sources of Stannary Law

Sir George Harrison said this peculiar system of jurisprudence is derived from:

> "the ancient customs and usages of the Stannaries, declared and confirmed, or altered from time to time, by Royal Charters, or by laws enacted in the British

---

14 Harrison, Sir George, *A Report of the Laws and Jurisdiction of the Stannaries* (1835) p 5

15 Resolution of Judges 1608 (See Appendix I for full text)

16 Pennington, R., *A History of the Mining Law of Cornwall and Devon* (1973) p 9

Legislature, or in the Stannary Convocations or Parliaments." [17]

Professor Pennington states Stannary Law developed from three sources:

"Cornish, Anglo-Saxon and Norman. The customary Cornish Law became amalgamated with the Customary Law of the Anglo-Saxons which Norman law then tolerated." [18]

Dr John Rowe stated simply Stannary Law had as one of its origins Celtic customary law.[19]

The body of customary law was added to by enactments of the Convocations of Tinners of Cornwall and the Great Court of the Devon Tinners, about which more shortly. In addition there were the Acts of the Westminster Parliament, for example, the Stannaries Act 1641, parts of which the Stannary Courts simply ignored, the Stannaries Courts Act 1836, which extended the jurisdiction of the Stannary Courts to matters connected with all Metals and Metallic Minerals in Cornwall in the same way as previously applied to tin, and the Stannaries Courts (Abolition) Act 1896 (as amended by the Constitutional Reform Act 2005[20]) which abolished the last Stannary Courts and transferred its jurisdiction. The abolition brought to end:

"the last remnant of a whole way of life in a county, or perhaps more accurately, country."[21]

17 Harrison, Sir George, *A Report of the Laws and Jurisdiction of the Stannaries* (1835) p 13

18 Pennington, R., *A History of the Mining Law of Cornwall and Devon* (1973) p 13

19 Rowe, J., *Cornwall in the Age of the Industrial Revolution* (1953 2nd Edition 1993) p 195

20 Constitutional Reform Act 2005 Schedule 4 section 17

21 Cruickshanks, E., "The Convocation of the Stannaries of Cornwall" (1986) *Parliaments, Estates and Representation* Vol 6 Part 1 p 67

Like English law Stannary law was based on precedent. Decisions of lower Stannary Courts were bound by decisions of higher Stannary Courts. Finally and significantly there were the various Charters.

The Charters

The foundation upon which rests the rights and privileges of the Stannaries are the Charters as follows:

- Charter of Liberties to the Tinners of Cornwall and Devon (1201);
- Charter of Liberties to the Tinners of Cornwall (1305);
- Charter of Confirmation to the Tinners of Cornwall (1402); and
- Grant or Patent of Pardon and Immunities to the Tinners, Bounders and Possessor of Works of Tin of Cornwall (1508).

The Charters are set out in full in Appendix I.

There was a minor Charter granted in 1466 which gave certain rights to Cornish Tinners in the Royal Forest of Dartmoor.

Sir George Harrison states "Those Charters merely confirmed pre-existing rights and privileges even then of ancient date".[22] Furthermore, he said the Charters of 1201 and 1305 demonstrated:

"that the system was not only in existence but even at the date of the earliest of those Charters it had, probably for centuries been established on the firm basis of prescriptive usage." [23]

22 Harrison, Sir George, *A Report of the Laws and Jurisdiction of the Stannaries* (1835) p 67

23 Harrison, Sir George, *A Report of the Laws and Jurisdiction of the Stannaries* (1835) p 67

The 1201 Charter confirmed the ancient privileges o bounding, of fuel and water and removed tinners from pleas of serfs.[24] No magistrate had jurisdiction over them save their Warden who alone or through his officers might summon them for civil and criminal matters.

The Charter of 1305 partially separated the Devon Stannaries from the Cornish Stannaries. It confirmed the right to bounding, freed tinners from ordinary taxation, confirmed the practice of tin coinage and tried to give precision to the jurisdiction of the Warden.

The 1201 and 1305 Charters, which placed criminal and civil jurisdiction over tinners in the hands of the Warden, resulted in the division of mining districts within Cornwall into a number of distinct provinces or Stannaries those being Foweymore, Blackmore, Tywarnhayle, Penwith and Kerrier. Each district was presided over by the Warden's representative, a Steward.

The 1305 Charter is the most significant of the charters and provided:

> "that all tinners… working those Stannaries, shall be free and quit of pleas of natives, and of all pleas and suits in anywise touching the Court of us, or of our heirs so they shall not answer before any justices or ministers of us or our heirs… except for pleas of land and of life and of members…"

It exempted tinners from:

> "tallages *(arbitrary taxes imposed by the king on the tenants of his demesne lands and on boroughs holding royal charters, or by a feudal lord on his tenants)* toll *(or charges for the use of markets, roads, bridges and other facilities)* stallages *(charges for the use*

---

24 State of being born in bondage or serfdom

r place in a market town for the sale of goods) aids
*ts exacted by the kings or a feudal lord from his
ist with occasional heavy expenditure)* and other
customs whatsoever; in the towns ports fairs and
markets within the county aforesaid."

It goes on to say:

"if any tinner transgressed in anything for which they
ought to be imprisoned... and in our prison of Lostwithiel and not elsewhere shall be kept and detained..."

In summary by the 1305 Charter "working miners" or
"privileged tinners" were not to be brought before the ordinary
Courts except upon charges of serious crime (murder,
manslaughter and mayhem). In all other matters concerning
tin mining or not, tinners were to sue and be sued in Stannary
Courts. So one sees, for example, cases of debt, contract,
assault and battery, defamation and trespass of swine amongst
other matters being heard before Stannary Courts. Lewis
called the 1305 Charter "the real constitution of the
Stannaries."[25]

The rights granted by the Charters have not been abrogated.

The independence of the Stannary system

It was clearly decided in the leading case of *Trewynard v Killigrew*
(1562)[26], during the reign of Elizabeth I, there was no appeal
from the Stannary Courts to the "ordinary Courts" of England.
A decision confirmed in Star Chamber in *Trewynnard v
Roscarrack* (1564) and *Langworthy v Scott* (1616).[27] As stated by
Lord Coke in 1608:

25 Lewis, G R., *The Stannaries: A Study of the Medieval Tin Miners of Cornwall and Devon*
    (1908) p 39

26 *Trewynard v Killigrew* (1562) (4 and 7 Elizabeth I)

27 *Trewynnard v Roscarrack* (1564) (4 Coke's Institutes 229); *Langworth v Scott* (1616)
    (3 Bulstr 183)

"Appeals first to the Steward of Stannary Court then Under Warden... then to Prince's Privy Council and not examinable in this Court or any other Court." [28]

Final appeal within the Stannary system was to the Privy Council of the Duke of Cornwall and then the Sovereign's Privy Council. Prince Albert, as Lord Warden of the Stannaries, gave many judgements in cases appealed to the Prince's Council.

Sir John Dodridge writing in 1650 described the system well:

"In every of which Stannaries, there is a Court, to minister Justice, in all causes personal arising between Tinner and Tinner, and between Tinner and Foreigner; and also the right of ownership of Tin Mines, and the disposition thereof; except in causes of Land, Life and Member: and if in any false and unjust Judgement be given in any of there said Courts, the Party aggrieved may make his Appeal unto the Lord-Warden of the Stannaries, who is their superior Judge, both for Law and Equity; and from him, unto the Body of the Council of the Lord Prince, Duke of Cornwall; to which the Duke the Stannaries are given, as by the former Charters have appeared; and from the Appeal lieth to the King's most Royal Person".[29]

Territorial jurisdiction of the Stannaries

In a Privy Council decision of 1632 it was stated:

"We cannot but discern but that the Stannaries extend over the whole County of Cornwall. The exemption of

28 Resolution of the Judges 1608 (See Appendix D)
29 Dodridge, Sir John, *An Historical Account of the Ancient and Modern State of the Principality of Wales Dutchy of Cornwall and Earldom of Chester* (1714)

tinners from toll is over the whole county. The power to dig and search for tin is over the whole county…" [30]

In this Cornwall differed from Devon and other areas which had mining laws. The Stannary system extended over the whole of Cornwall and was not limited to particular areas as with Devon.

Who were tinners within the jurisdiction of the Stannaries?

A "tinner" who could prove he came within the jurisdiction of the Stannaries enjoyed certain rights and privileges. He could only sue and be sued in Stannary Courts. Warrants and writs against tinners from non Stannary Courts were not allowed and officers attempting to serve them were liable to arrest. There was no appeal from Stannary Courts to the "ordinary" courts of England. Only a "tinner" who came within the jurisdiction of the Stannaries, a "privileged tinner", could claim the benefits of the Charters particularly the Charter of 1305. This situation created tensions. Many claimed to be "privileged tinners" to bring themselves within the jurisdiction of the Stannaries. Sir George Harrison, quoting a Charter of Henry VII gives the following example:

> "As for *Contywall use*, it appeerth by very mayn instances, that Earles, Lords, Abbotts, other Clergie-men, some Judges, Women, etc., did sue in the Stannaryes as *'Stannatores'*…"[31]

In addition the Stannary Courts were jealous of their jurisdiction and sought to extend it.

---

30 Resolution of the Privy Council 1632—Order 21st January 1632 (See Appendix I)

31 Harrison, Sir George, *Substance of a Report on the Laws and Jurisdiction of the Stannaries in Cornwall* (1835) p 133

Two questions arise. The first concerned the definition of "tinner". Did it, as the Stannaries claimed, include not only manual labourers, but their employers, the holders of shares in tin mines, the dealers in tin and in ore, and all the artisan classes connected with tin mining? Or was it to comprise only working miners, and only as long as they remained in work? [32]

Many attempts were made to determine the class of "privileged tinners" who came within the ambit of the Stannaries. The Convocation Act (Cornwall) 1588 section 7 passed by the Convocation of the Tinners of Cornwall declared that:

> "there are two sorts of tinners, viz, the tin worker, spalliard (*a pickman or working miner*) or pyoner (*a form of adventurer*)... (who) is not to sue or to be sued out of the Courts of Stannary... except (for) matters touching land, life or mayhem"; and
>
> "the second sort of tinner (who) are such as have some part or portion of tinworks, or receive toll tin either as lords or farmers thereof, or do convert (*smelt*) black tin into white tin, or are necessary for getting or obtaining tin, as colliers, blowers, carpenters, smiths, tin merchants and such like intermeddling with traffic of tin... (they) may sue and implead (or) be sued or impleaded in the Stannary Courts."

The wonderfully named "Act against the divers incroachments and Oppressions in the Stannary Courts", otherwise the Stannaries Act 1641 passed by the Westminster Parliament stated at section 3 in defining "privileged tinners", that the:

> "great liberties do of Right belong to the working Tinner, working without Fraud or Deceit in the

Stannaries aforesaid, and not to any other nor elsewhere working…"

and not to those who:

"for small or no Consideration (have) sought and acquired… decayed tin-works and small and inconsiderable Parts in the same and other tin-works."

The Stannary Act 1641 also defines, at section 4, a "privileged tinner" "is or shall be working". The Stannary Courts ignored the Stannaries Act 1641 Act see, for example, the Stannary Court case of *Tregilgas v Dingey* (1843) in which the Court decided that a shareholder in a tin mining company was a "privileged tinner". Persuasive legal opinion is that the Stannary Courts continued to exercise a jurisdiction for over 200 years after that power had been removed from it.

John Tregonning in his book "Laws of the Stannaries" in answer to the question who is a "privileged tinner" states:

"the spalliard working with pick and shovel, the waterman, the boll or barrow-man, the dresser, the blower, and all other tinner-labourer and workmen, that necessarily attend getting tin, or the dressing, blowing, or whitening it, so long as they continue working without fraud, are properly called privileged tinners…"[33]

In the same book he defines a tinner as:

"labouring tinner, a blower, owner of blowing-houses, a spalliard, or adventurer that is at any charge for getting or making of tin, a smith, a collier, or any person that is employed in working or making any tin for the working of the same…"

33 Tregonning, J., *The Laws of the Stannaries of Cornwall with Marginal Notes* (1808) p 39

The Stannaries Act 1836 extended the authority of the Stannary Courts providing:

> all adventurers, agents, labourers connected in any way with mines either supplying materials or otherwise were held to be miners and made to sue or be sued in the Stannary."

Thus the jurisdiction extended to any mine worked for lead, copper or other metal or metallic mineral or the searching or working smelting or purifying any lead copper or other metallic mineral as fully as with respect to tin or tin mines. It also extended to non-metallic minerals found in the same mine and worked by the same adventurers. So, for example, workers in the china clay industry could be held to be tinners see: *Re Treverbyn Trevanion Clay Works* (1872)[34] and *Pearce v Grundy* (1818).[35] See also the case of *Boscawen v Chaplin* (1536)[36] towards the end of the reign of Henry VIII in which the parties were described as tinners who were a:

> "wise man and learned in law of this Realm and a merchant buyer of tin."

Note in addition *Trewynard v Killigrew* (1562)[37] in which the parties are said to be "esquires and gentlemen."

Bainbridge in his "A treatise on the Law of Mines and Minerals" defines "privileged tinners" as:

> "labouring tinners, dressers, smelters and all persons actually employed in tin works" while "all officers of the

---

34 *Re: Treverbyn Trevanion Clay Works* (1872) Reported Royal Institute of Cornwall Gazette 1st June 1872

35 *Pearce v Grundy* (1818) decided by Vice Warden of the Stannaries 7th April 1818

36 *Boscawen v Chaplin* (1536) (Harleian Manuscripts 6380 folio 9)

37 Trewynard v Killigrew (1562) (4 and 7 Elizabeth)

Court, owners of tin works, adventurers, purchasers of tin, and all other that intermeddle with tin are called 'tinners at large'."[38]

The "privileged tinner" could only sue or be sued in his own Stannary Court. While tinners at large could be sued by "foreigners" (strangers to the Stannaries) in local Courts at the election of the plaintiff. Thus the distinction between a "privileged tinner" and a "tinner at large" was important. Most significantly only a "privileged tinner" could claim the benefits of the Charter of 1305.

Stannary Law—Extent of Jurisdiction

The system of law governing tin mining was universal in that it related not only to operations and transactions necessarily occurring in the industries but also extended to all aspects of the lives of those who were engaged in tin affairs. The number of people this encompassed was very substantial. The 1201 Charter provided no magistrate or coroner had jurisdiction except the Warden of the Stannaries who had plenary power "to do them justice, and to hold them to law".

It is clear from the 1201 Charter the Stannary Courts exercised a criminal jurisdiction otherwise why provide exceptions of "murder manslaughter and mayhem" or "land life and members" sometimes called "life land and mayhem". The Charters have been interpreted to mean the exclusion of "land, life and limb" meaning the Lord Warden could exercise jurisdiction over claims for damages in respect of loss of life or physical injury and could not order capital punishment or mutilation but could order lesser punishments.

The Stannaries had two prisons, one in Lydford (nineteenth-century Lidford) in Devon and the other in Lostwithiel in Cornwall. The Stannary Courts of Devon acquired the

---

38 Bainbridge, W., *A Treatise on the law of Mines and Minerals* (1856) p 571

nickname of "Lidford Law" after "a judge of the Stannary Devonshire who, having hanged a felon among the tinners in the forenoon, sat in judgement on him in the afternoon".[39, 40] It is certainly the case the Stannary Courts were notorious for their partiality. Richard Carew reported in 1602 that witnesses gave evidence:

> "rather for serving a turn than for manifesting a truth, and that the jurors' verdict hath savoured more of affection than reason, especially in controversies grown between strangers and some of the parts..."[41]

The Court rolls record criminal offences of theft, riotous assembly, forcible entry on land, wrongful levying of hue and cry and so on. Lewis gives a graphic description of the cases heard:

> "Trespassing with swine and geese on a neighbour's cornfield, cutting another's timber, infractions of the size of beer, baking unwholesome bread and, shortly after the Black Death, evasions of the Statute of Labourers. Instances are not lacking of an entire parish being fined for failure to repairs its roads."[42]

A. L. Rowse gave further examples of the extent of the jurisdiction exercised by the Stannary Courts:

---

39 "Lidford Law" *Devon and Cornwall Notes and Gleanings* (April 1888) p 62, quoting Adams, T., *Lycanthropy* (1615) p. 28. See also John Chynoweth *Tudor Cornwall* (2002) p 284 which dates the term from 1399.

40 There is a contradiction which as far as I know has not been researched. While the 1201 Charter has always been taken to mean the Stannary Courts could not order capital punishment yet it is clear that on occasion they did precisely that.

41 Quoted in John Chynoweth *Tudor Cornwall* (2002) p 285

42 Lewis, G. R., *The Stannaries: A Study of the Medieval Tin Miners of Cornwall and Devon* (1908 Reprint 1965) pp 119-120

Parliamentary privilege thus has its origins in a case in which a Stannary Court exercised its jurisdiction which required an Act of Parliament to reverse its decision.

Bounding

Lewis described "the solemn mystery of the art of bounding"[45] as:

> "freely searching for tin wherever it might be suspected regardless of the rights of the landlord…"[46]

The 1305 Charter provided:

> "We have granted also the said tinners that they may dig tin, and turves to melt tin, anywhere in the lands, moors, and wastes of us, and of others whosoever; in the county aforesaid, and divert water and water courses for the works of the Stannaries aforesaid…"

The Victoria History of the Counties of England of 1906 explained:

> "Cornish Law, after excluding highways, houses, and churchyards from devastation, allowed any man to dig for tin in all wastrel, *(Terris vastis et moris -1305 Charter— wastrel lands and moorland)*, and in enclosed lands, if the latter were of the duchy manors, or had been anciently bounded and assured for wastrel. Anywhere else the owner's consent was required.
>
> The bounds were tracts of land enjoyed by their possessors in respect of tin only, and the ceremony of taking a claim was the digging of a small pit, and making of a small pile of turf at each of the corners of

---

45 Concanen, G., *A Report of a Trial at Bar Rowe v Brenton* (1830) p xxxiv

46 Lewis, G R., *The Stannaries: A Study of the Medieval Tin Miners of Cornwall and Devon* (1908) p 35

the plot. This had to be repeated each year else the bounds were said to have lapsed. The laws of the Stannaries contain no provision regulating the amount of land which might be included in a pair of bounds, and a possible outcome of this omission is seen by the fact that in 1786 all Dartmoor comprising 5,000 acres were taken by a single bounder. Nor has there ever been any definition of the work necessary to hold the bounds, with the possible exception of one which made toll tin obligatory at the end of the third year else the land reverted to its lord. The taking up of new bounds as well as renewing of old bounds had after 1495 to be reported to the nearest Stannary Court *(now Truro County Court)*, where having been proclaimed at the three following sessions in default of opposition the bounders title became valid."[47]

Possibly the most succinct description is given in Halsbury's Laws of England:

"The ownership of a mine vests prima facie in the owner of the freehold. This right is, however, modified by the custom of tin bounding. The custom has fallen into disuse, but it has never been abrogated. Under the custom, if a tin mine lay within waste land or certain inclosed land and was not worked by the surface owner, a tinner could claim and, if various conditions were met, be granted tin bounds. The grant carried the exclusive right to search for and work all tin and tin ore within the bounds, subject to a payment to the owner of the soil."[48]

---

47 Page, W., (Ed.) *The Victoria History of the Counties of England Cornwall* (1906) p 526
48 Halsbury's Laws of England Mines Minerals and Quarries (Volume 31) section 10 para. 589

There was a set procedure which involved corner bounds or side bounds. Bounds are required to have four corners and to be defined by twenty four turfs or stones, six to each corner. Every bounder is required to proclaim at the next Stannary Court (now Truro County Court) the date of his possession, names of his partners and the person who cut the bound and the limits. The same proclamation must be made in the two following Court sessions. Three months notice in writing prior to cutting must be given to the owner of the soil who may then choose to cut bounds. Bounds must be annually renewed and must be worked. If a miner successfully bounded land he acquired a right against the lord and it was that right which was commonly called bounds.

Coinage

A tax known as 'coinage' and said to have been in existence since 1198, was paid on all smelted tin. It was ended by Cromwell and re-introduced by Charles II. Coinage became more elaborate and complicated over the years but was not finally abolished until 1838.[49] By the same Act the customs duty on imported foreign tin was reduced. The Stannaries thus lost the benefit of a high protective tariff and it was felt impossible to leave them saddled with coinage duties.[50]

There were different rates of coinage levied on tin produced in Cornwall and Devon, for example, in 1198 it was 60 pence per thousand weight in Cornwall and 30 pence in Devon. An additional duty of one mark per thousandweight was then imposed making 22 old pennies per hundredweight in Cornwall and 19 old pence per hundredweight in Devon.[51] In 1838 the Duchy of Cornwall[52] was awarded an annuity of

---

49 Coinage Abolition Act 1838

50 TNA T 38/837—Civil List Notes (1897)

51 Pennington, R., "Stannary Law" (1988) *Bulletin of the Peak District Historical Society* Vol. 10, No 4

52 There was at this time no Duke of Cornwall so the Duchy was managed by the

£16,216 15s 0d (approx £1.1 million in 2011) in exchange for surrendering its coinage duty. No allowance was made for inflation and the figure remained unchanged until 1983 when it was abolished.[53]

Coinage was payable at 'coinage towns': Lostwithiel, Liskeard, Truro, Helston, Bodmin and Penzance.

The Duke also had the right to purchase all tin, or pre-emption, which was only rarely exercised.

Crown.
53 Miscellaneous Financial Provisions Act 1983

Chapter 2

The Convocation of the Tinners of Cornwall

"no other institution has had such wide powers in the history of this country"[54]

Introduction

The Convocation of the Stannaries of Cornwall, from now on the Convocation, was (*and, arguably, remains*) a remarkable institution. It did not make Cornwall unique: Devon Tinners also had a "Parliament" as did the lead miners of Derbyshire and the Mendip Hills but it did, for reasons that shall now be explained, make Cornwall different.

The Convocation of the Tinners of Cornwall and its equivalent in Devon, the Great Court of the Tinners of Devon, were unusual in that they were representative legislatures linked to a single industry.[55] The Convocations were not assemblies concerned with the people of a specific area like, for example, the Scottish or Westminster Parliaments. However the Cornish Convocation in particular could claim to be occupied with a significant portion of the population since, as was explained in the previous chapter, the number of people who could claim to be tinners was very wide.

They were, possibly, an expansion of, and an offshoot from, the grand juries of the Stannary Courts. It is said in some older

---

54 Laws of the Stannaries—Trevithick Society (1974) Introduction

55 Cruickshanks, E., "The Convocation of the Stannaries of Cornwall" (1986) *Parliaments, Estates and Representation* Vol 6 No 1 p 59

local histories that until 1305 the tinners of Devon and Cornwall met in one Parliament on Hingston Hill near Callington; others suggest Crockernton on Dartmoor. After the Charter of 1305 the Parliaments were held separately.[56]

The Rev. Richard Polwhele claimed:

> "I have scarcely have any doubt but the Stannary parliaments in this place were a continuation, even to our own times, of the old British courts before the time of Julius Caesar; those Stannary parliaments were similar, in every point of resemblance, to the old British courts."[57]

The records for Devon date back to 1520 while those for Cornwall to 1588.[58]

Professor Robert Pennington asserted:

> "The Parliament of the Convocation of the Tinners of Cornwall was a unique institution in that it was not only a body representative of a special industrial and commercial sector of the economy, but was also a legislature with powers parallel to those of the Parliament at Westminster and had power to veto legislation by the central government if it affected tin mining. *No other institution has ever had such wide powers in the history of this country.*" (emphasis added)[59]

The remarkable power of veto possessed by the Convocation distinguished Cornwall from other areas, like Devon, who could also claim a "miners' parliament".

---

56 Carew, R., *The Survey of Cornwall* (1602) p 16

57 Polwhele, Rev Richard, *The History of Cornwall* (1816) p 92

58 Pennington, R., "Stannary Law" (1988) *Bulletin of the Peak District Mines Historical Society* Vol 10 No 4

59 Laws of the Stannaries—Trevithick Society (1974) Introduction

The 1508 Charter

The recorded history of the Convocation of Cornwall begins with the Charter of 1508 (See Appendix I) granted by Henry VII. The background to the granting of the Charter is as follows. In 1497 the Cornish rebelled against Henry VII. This was one of six uprisings which occurred over a one hundred and fifty year period; the others being in 1548, 1549, 1642 and 1648. The immediate causes of dissatisfaction were increases in taxation to finance an unpopular war with Scotland, the suspension of the Stannaries in 1496 and stricter rules being imposed by the then Duke of Cornwall, Prince Arthur, on tin bounding and coinage. There was, initially, an unexpectedly successful march on London led by Michael Angove and Thomas Flamank. However, the rebels were defeated by the King's forces in Blackheath and the leaders executed. Henry VII was surprisingly moderate in the way he dealt with the uprising, presumably not wishing to make a bad situation worse. A number of pardons were issued and property previously confiscated was restored. Equally significant was the Charter of Pardon:

> "a move clearly designed to win pacification and renewed accommodation of Cornwall not only by restoring the Stannaries (on the payment of a £1000 fine) but also enhancing the constitutional status of the Stannary Parliament. Both the privileges of the tinners and the legislative capacity of the Parliament.... Coming so soon after the crisis of 1497, this must be seen as a deliberate strategy to restore the constitutional accommodation of Cornwall. The Charter of Pardon extended the definition of tinner (and thus the jurisdiction of Stannary Law) to include almost anyone connected in one way or another with the tin trade"[60]

60 Payton, P., *Cornwall—A History* (2004) p 115

The Charter provided that the Convocation of the Tinners of Cornwall consisted of:

> "twenty four good and lawful men of the four Stannaries of the county of Cornwall, namely six men from each of the Stannaries elected and appointed from time to time as occasion requires…"

The four Stannaries were centred on the principal mining districts of (1) Penwith and Kerrier, which comprised Land's End, the Lizard peninsula and area between Hayle, Redruth and Helston (2) Tywarnhaile which ran from Truro to Penryn in the east and to St. Agnes in the West (3) Blackmore, which corresponded with Hensborrow granite boss and (4) Foyemore which extended over Bodmin moor. Writs would be issued to the mayors of the four "coinage towns" 1) Launceston for Foyemore 2) Lostwithiel for Blackmore 3) Truro for Tywarnhaile and 4) Helston for Penwith. The electorate consisted of the freeholders of each of the Stannaries who elected six Stannators making twenty four in all. Latterly each Stannator was empowered to nominate an Assistant who acted in a consultative capacity and as a link to the free miners.

Convocations of the Tinners of Cornwall were held to enact legislation met in 1588, 1624, 1636, 1686 to 1688, 1704, 1750 and 1752 to 1753. There was an attempt to arrange a meeting of the Convocation in 1835 and there was some lobbying again in 1865. Neither was successful.

Henry VII stated that he would ask Parliament to ratify the Charter but he died before he had the chance so to do. This does not mean, as is sometimes suggested, that because the Charter was not ratified by Parliament it is not legally enforceable. At this time the most typical means of creating new law was by Royal Charter.[61]

---

61 As a contemporary example see the suggestion that the recommendations of

The Procedures of the Convocation

The Convocation of the Tinners of Cornwall would be summoned (for example of the summons see Appendix II) by the Duke of Cornwall, or if no Duke, by the monarch, whereupon the Lord Warden of the Stannaries issued precepts to the four "coinage towns", to hold elections for Stannators. The Stannators latterly appointed twenty four assistants, who formed a lower house to assist them and advise on legislation.

The Lord Warden gave a speech to the Stannators who then elected a Speaker, who having been approved by the Lord Warden, appointed the necessary officials and then opened the session. The Lord Warden and Vice Warden of the Stannaries were excluded. Eventually sixteen Stannators formed a binding majority. The Convocation had the right to initiate legislation concerning the Stannaries, as well as to ratify proposals by the Lord Warden.

John Thomas, Vice Warden of the Stannaries from 1783 until 1812, stated in a report of 1785 that the Convocation:

> "is like unto the British in this respect that it consists of three branches viz The Lord Warden, representing the King; 24 Stannators representing the Lords and twenty four assistants chosen by the Stannators, the Commons."[62]

G R Lewis stated the Convocation operated in manner:

> "scarcely different from Westminster." [63]

---

the Leveson enquiry into the Press be implemented by means of a Royal Charter.

62 Thomas, John, Vice Warden of the Stannaries—*Report to the Princes Council 21st February 1785*

63 Lewis, G R., *The Stannaries: A Study of the Medieval Tin Miners of Cornwall and Devon* (1908) p 128

The right of veto

The 1508 Charter provides:

> "no statutes, acts, ordinances… or proclamations *(statute, actus, ordinaciones, provisiones, restrictions sive proclamaciones)* made at any time hereafter shall be put into force in the said county (Cornwall) to prejudice or burdening of the said tinners bounders, possessors of tin works… proprietors of blowing houses… buyers of black or white tin or dealers in white tin or the heirs and successors of any them" unless a Convocation… had been convened and given its consent."

The right of veto applied to enactments of the monarch in Privy Council, the Duke of Cornwall in the Prince's Council as well as Acts of the Westminster Parliament. The position, arguably, was and remains, that the consent of the Convocation is required before enactments of the Westminster Parliament are passed affecting tin mining, and latterly all mining, in Cornwall.[64]

Was the right of veto exercised?

It was exercised on at least three occasions. In 1674 there was a dispute between the Convocation and the King because the Convocation refused to delegate its contracting powers to a House of Commons Select Committee. In 1687 the Convocation refused to ratify a Royal Contract for pre-emption. The most notable occasion occurred during the reign of James II in 1686 when Letters Patent issued by Charles II appointing Penzance as a coinage town was nullified. The Cornish Convocation of Tinners declared they had taken "no Notice" of the order.[65]

---

64 Professor Robert Pennington Letter to Daily Telegraph 15th June 1974

65 Pearce, T., *The Laws and Customs of the Stannaries of the Counties of Devon and Cornwall* (1725)

Chapter 3

Does Stannary Law have any modern application?

Introduction

Andrew George, M.P. on 29 March 2007 asked the following question in Parliament:

> "To ask the Minister of State, Department of Constitutional Affairs (1) what distinct constitutional status applies (a) to Cornwall, (b) Isles of Scilly (c) the Cornish people, (d) the Duchy of Cornwall (e) the Council of the Isles of Scilly (f) Cornish Stannary organisations and (g) any other Cornish or Duchy based institution which does not apply to England…"

Bridget Prentice, M.P., Parliamentary Under Secretary of State at the Department of Constitutional Affairs, responded:

> "On the question about Stannary organisations, there are no valid Cornish Stannary organisations in existence. It is noted that Stannary courts were abolished under the Stannaries Court (Abolition) Act 1896."[66]

On 29 May 2009 Mr. George tabled another question:

---

66 HC Written Answers 29th March 2007 Column 1673W

"To ask the Secretary of State for Justice, with reference to the Answer of 29th March 2007, Official Report, column 1673 on politics and government: South West Region, whether any parts of Stannary Law still exists as part of the Law of England."

The answer provided by Mr Michael Wills M.P., Minister of State at the Ministry of Justice, was:

"The body of Stannary customary law has not been systematically repealed. It is likely however that such customary law has been superseded by modern legislation. There were also provisions in 19th Century primary legislation relating to the Stannaries but these have largely been repealed."[67]

More recently, on 3 May 2011 Lord Laird made the following enquiry:

"To ask Her Majesty's Government, in a legal context, what is the status of Stannary law in Cornwall."[68]

The reply on 11 May 2011 from Lord McNally, Minister of State, Ministry of Justice was:

"Cornwall is subject to UK legislation. While the body of Stannary law has not been systematically repealed, it is likely that such customary law has been superseded by modern legislation."[69]

---

67 HC Written Answers 29th May 2009 Column 1451W
68 HL Written Questions 3rd May 2011 Column HL8818
69 HL Written Answers 11 May 2011 Column WA214

The views expressed by Ms. Prentice, Mr. Wills and Lord McNally are challengeable. It is arguable the Convocation of the Tinners of Cornwall still, in theory, exists. Indisputably Stannary Law remains part of English Law. In fact, as has been explained, Stannary Law, did not, as the answers from Mr. Wills and Lord McNally imply, consist solely of "customary law": it was also based on Charters, Convocation Acts, Acts of the Parliament at Westminster and precedent. The body of Stannary Law has not been abolished although it has much less relevance today.

Significant Court Cases

R v East Powder Magistrates Court ex parte Lampshire (1979)[70]

The facts are that on 23 October 1977 Mr Reginald Brian Hambly used a motor vehicle on a public road in St Austell for which a licence under the Vehicle (Excise) Act 1971 was not in force. Mr. Hambly was summoned to appear before the East Powder Magistrates on 15 June 1978. The Magistrates decided they had no jurisdiction to hear the case because Mr. Hambly claimed to be a "privileged tinner" and elected to be tried in a court exercising Stannary jurisdiction. A judicial review was sought by Ms. Lampshire who was an officer of the Motor Taxation Department in Cornwall.

The opinion of Counsel[71] instructed by Mr. Hambly said his claim required proof:

a) That he was a "privileged tinner";
b) That Fore Street St Austell is within a vill, tithing or hamlet where some tin work is situate;

---

70 *R v East Powder Magistrates' Court ex parte Lampshire* (1979) (2 All ER 329)
71 Brian Galgin 1 Harcourt Buildings 3rd March 1978

c) that a vehicle excise is a "toll or charge for the use of the road" within the Charter of 1305;

d) The Stannary Courts retained a criminal jurisdiction which was transferred by the Stannary Courts (Abolition) Act 1896 to the Cornwall County Court; and

e) That a "privileged tinner" was entitled to insist on being tried in that County Court.

Counsel continued that Mr. Hambly needed to establish that he was a "privileged tinner" *before* the date of the summons but not at the date when the offence was committed. He then went on to say, in his view, a Road Fund License was a charge for the use of the road, however, whether it was a "toll" within the meaning of the 1305 Charter was open to debate. The word within the Charter of 1305 suggests a local charge, however, the use of the word *thelonia* (customs) (equivalent to *vectigalia* (revenue, tribute)) relates to any charge made by the State for the use of land which would include a tax for use of land as a road. Counsel's opinion was that if Mr. Hambly could show he was entitled to take advantage of the 1305 Charter he was exempt from vehicle license duty.

On behalf of Ms. Lampshire it was argued in the High Court before Lord Widgery C.J., Kilner Brown and Robert Goff JJ on 12/13 December 1978, that criminal jurisdiction had not been exercised by the Stannary Courts since 1783 and probably long before. That the Charter of 1305 had granted privileges only as to civil rights and such criminal jurisdiction as had been exercised had been that of a "court leet" (a customary court) which had been abolished. Counsel also said despite various nineteenth century cases desuetude[72] can end a jurisdiction.

For Mr. Hambly it was argued that it was clear that criminal cases had been heard before the Stannary Courts. All tinners working in the Stannaries were to be free of "quit of pleas of

---

72 The doctrine by which a law or treaty is rendered obsolete because of disuse

naifty *(state of being born in bondage or serfdom)* and were not to answer before any justices on plea arising within the Stannaries except pleas of "land, life and limb". The exception showed other crimes were included. Furthermore it was argued desuetude did not apply and various cases were quoted in support of the argument.

Lord Widgery said:

> "the prosecution accepted (Mr. Hambly) was a "privileged tinner" and the fact *the rights of tinners had been in abeyance did not destroy them…*" (emphasis added)
>
> "For my part I have found this a simple case because it seems to me that Parliament being supreme and Parliament have enacted… (various Acts)… there can be no conclusion left beyond the fact that the nominees of Parliament—the justices—are put in a position they can try a summary offence of this kind even though committed within the Stannaries."

Judge Robert Goff said "the respondent (Mr. Hambly) is a privileged tinner."

In one sense the answer they arrived at was straightforward. The Judges seem to have accepted that the Stannary Courts had exercised a criminal jurisdiction. That the criminal jurisdiction they had exercised was that of a customary "court leet" whose jurisdiction had lapsed or that various Acts of the Westminster Parliament had displaced that jurisdiction. Thus the case was referred back to the Magistrates for a determination. The decision of the High Court was not appealed and the verdict stands that while the Stannaries Courts (Abolition) Act 1896 may have transferred the civil jurisdiction of the Stannary Courts to the County Courts it did not transfer a criminal jurisdiction. The Judges never questioned the 1201 or 1305 Charters or the fact that certain rights were granted to "privileged tinners".

They did not direct their minds to whether a vehicle excise license is a "toll or charge for the use of the road" within the Charter of 1305. This was not a question the court was asked to address.

Frederick Richard Albert Trull v Restormel Borough Council (1994)[73]

Mr. Trull argued he was not due to pay rates because he was a tinner and because the Westminster Parliament had no jurisdiction to enact laws for those within Cornwall which would in any way impinge on the rights or privileges granted to tinners except with the approval of the "Cornish Parliament". In any event, he went on, those obligations could only be enforced in Stannary Courts.

Mr Trull's arguments were rejected. Cornwall was part of the United Kingdom and Mr. Trull was due to pay the rates although it was accepted he was a tinner.

Bounding

Despite what is said in Halsbury's, quoted in Chapter one it is still possible to bound. Application is made to Truro County Court which will issue the appropriate court orders.

Does the Convocation still exist as a legal institution?

The answer, debatably, is yes for the following reasons. The English legal system, unlike that of Scotland, does not generally recognize the principle of "desuetude" by which statutes, legislation or legal principles lapse and become unenforceable by long habit of non-enforcement. There are a number of cases which demonstrate this point:

Rex v The Mayor and Jurats of Hasting (1822)[74]

Despite the fact that a Court had not been held since 1790 the Mayor was obliged to hold a Court.

---

73 *Frederick Richard Albert Trull v Restormel Borough Council* (1994 WL 1062112)
74 *Rex v Mayor and Jurats of Hastings* (1822) (1 Dowl & Ry. 148)

Rex v The Steward and Suitors of the Manor of Havering Atte Bower (1822)[75]

It was decided the fact that there was non-user for fifty years had not deprived them of the power of holding a Court for the recovery of debts.

The side note of the report of the case says:

> "Held, that this Court, being for the public benefit, the words of permission in the charter were obligatory; and that the right of determining suits was not lost by non-user."

Rex v The Mayor and Corporation of Wells (1836)[76]

The particular Court in question had not been held for two hundred years. There were no funds for holding the Court and no one knew the procedures. The judge, Patteson J, said:

> "I do not think I have any discretion on the subject. The power to hold this Court being granted by the charter, I do not think that the corporation can lay it aside merely on the grounds of want of funds; as to length of time, I cannot distinguish between fifty-two years in the case cited and two hundred."

Attorney General of the Isle of Man v Cowley and Kinrade (1859)[77]

It was stated:

> "Were any Court lawfully possesses a jurisdiction for the benefit of the subject in the administration of justice, it is settled that mere non user does not take it away."

75 *Rex v Steward of Havering* (1822) (2 Dowl. & Ry 176n)
76 *Rex v Wells Corporation* (1836) (4 Dowl. 562)
77 *Attorney General of Isle of Man v Cowley and Kinrade* (1859) (12 Moore PCC)

Manchester Corporation v Manchester Palace of Varieties (1955)[78]

This case involved the use or misuse of a coat of arms. It was heard in front of the High Court of Chivalry which has absolute jurisdiction in such matters. The fact the Court had not sat for two hundred years was no bar to its sitting. It is clear should a similar case arise in the future the Court could again sit.

Attorney General v H.R.H. Prince Ernest Augustus of Hanover (1957)[79]

This is a case of the sort which is thrown up from time to time and gives immense pleasure to the legal theorist. The matter arose from the Princess Sophia Naturalization Act 1705 which provided:

> "the said Princess and the issue of her body, and all persons lineally descending from her, born or hereafter to be born, be and shall be… deemed… natural born subjects of this kingdom."

Prince Ernest Augustus sought a declaration he was a British subject by virtue of the legislation. Initially the High Court held that the statute though perhaps not obsolete, was entirely spent. The Court of Appeal held the enacting words were plain and unambiguous;

> "that the fact by virtue of the passage of time since the statute was enacted the enacting words on their plain construction might lead to absurd and inconvenient results was no reason why the court should depart from the ordinary canons of construction."

---

78 *Manchester Corporation v Manchester Palace of Varieties Ltd* (1955) (2 WLR 440 1955) (1 All ER 387)

79 *Attorney General v HRH Prince Ernest Augustus of Hanover* (1957) (AC 436) ((2 WLR 1 1957)

Prince Ernest Augustus got his declaration. He was a British subject. The decision of the Court of Appeal was upheld by the House of Lords.

Royal Mines Act 1693

The above Act which still forms part of the law of England and Wales contains the following provision;

> "Provided always That nothing contained in this Act shall alter determine or make void the Charters granted to the Tinners of Devon and Cornwall by any of the Kings and Queens of this Realm or any of the Liberties Privileges or Franchises of the said Tinners or to alter determine or make void the Laws or Constitutions of the Stannaries of Devon or Cornwall or any of them."

Thus enshrined in an Act of Parliament is a recognition of the Laws and Constitution of the Stannaries."

Summary

There are, based on the precedents quoted above, convincing arguments that the Convocation of the Tinners of Cornwall and by extension the Great Court of the Devon Tinners still exist as legal institutions and could be summoned.

Has the right of veto been withdrawn?

Dafydd Wigley M.P. on 3 May 1977 asked the Attorney-General the following question:

> "on what date and by what enactment the provisions of the Charter of Pardon of the twenty-third year of the reign of Henry VII was rescinded or amended in relation to the Stannaries of Cornwall."

The Attorney General replied:

"My noble friend is making enquiries into this matter and will be writing to the Hon. Member."[80]

Mr Wigley received a reply from the Lord Chancellor, Lord Elwyn Jones, dated 14 May 1977 which did not directly answer the questions raised. The Lord Chancellor quoted from Professor Robert Pennington's Book "Stannary Law"[81] in which Pennington pointed out that Henry VII promised to have the Charter ratified by Act of Parliament but died before he could do so. Pennington suggested in his book that the question is in abeyance as to whether the Convocation could veto a Westminster Act of Parliament. It was also noted by the Lord Chancellor no doubt had ever been expressed about Parliament's power to enact legislation for the Stannaries without consent of the Convocation of the Tinners of Cornwall.

The Lord Chancellor then went on to say that: "no record would be noted against the original of any subsequent rescission or amendment."

Vetoing a Bill of the Westminster Parliament

It is a principle of English Law that the Courts did not hold an Act of Parliament ineffective once it had been passed. The view of the Courts is they are not competent to question the regularity or propriety of an Act of Parliament once it is on the Statute Roll. So once an Act of Parliament had been passed it is possible that the Cornish tin interests have no legal redress before a Court despite a breach by the Crown of its obligations embodied in the 1508 Charter. However if a Bill were to be introduced into Parliament which affected the Cornish tin mining industry the Convocation of the Tinners of Cornwall could, arguably, be summoned to exercise its veto.

---

80 HC Deb 3 May 1977 vol. 931 cc 114-5W
81 Pennington, Prof. R., *Stannary Law* (1973)

The opinion of Professor Pennington, expressed in a letter to the Daily Telegraph in 1974 was that:

> "it will undoubtedly be possible for interested Cornish-men to obtain a Court order directing the Duke of Cornwall and the Lord Warden to hold a Convocation to discover whether Cornwall consents..."[82]

to a Bill which would affect the tin mining interests.

The Ministry of Justice in a letter to the writer asserted as follows:

> "Notwithstanding any ancient prerogative instruments such as medieval Royal Charters, the United Kingdom Parliament is sovereign and in our view may legislate for the Stannaries without the assent of the former Stannary Parliament."[83]

The Ministry also said:

> "Although the Stannary Parliament has not been "abolished" by a formal set of legislation consideration of relevant cases by District Judge Duncan Adams some years ago suggest any rights of the Stannary Parliament had been superseded by all modern laws. The United Kingdom Parliament is the supreme legislative authority and has the power to repeal or modify any earlier statute or legislative instrument."

When a request was made to see the papers relating to the consideration of District Judge Adams the Ministry replied it did not have them. Enquiries suggest the Ministry of Justice is referring to a case in 2001 in Truro County Court whose records are not available.

---

82 Professor Robert Pennington letter to Daily Telegraph 24th May 1974.
83 Letter to writer from Ministry of Justice 28th August 2008

Conclusion

It is clear that although the Stannary Courts were abolished Stannary Law was not. While much of Stannary Law may not have any modern relevance there are parts which remain and are capable of application.

The right to "bound" can still be exercised and is from time to time. It remains possible to demonstrate that a person is a "privileged tinner" although the full extent of that term has not recently been explored. It can certainly be legitimately argued that, for example, clay mine workers are "privileged tinners". If "privileged tinners" exist then they still enjoy the rights of the Charters. Arguably even the possibility of not paying vehicle excise duties. The full extent of the benefits of the 1305 Charter has not been subject to judicial scrutiny for some time.

As for the Convocation of the Tinners of Cornwall there are many who misunderstand its application. It was a body which represented an industry not a population within a territory although the number of people who were engaged in that industry was significant. It extended, unlike the Great Court of the Tinners of Devon, over the whole of Cornwall. It also had the extraordinary right of veto which does differentiate Cornwall's Tinner's Parliament from similar bodies. Its methods of election by the standards of today are hardly democratic. However, it continues to have a resonance for some within Cornwall. An argument can be constructed that it still exists as a "legal institution" although that will become more and more difficult to sustain as time passes. If a case can be maintained that the Convocation of the Tinners of Cornwall exists then exactly the same logic would apply to the Great Court of the Tinners of Devon. However the question is not one of law it is one of politics. It is difficult to imagine a situation in which the Duke of Cornwall would summon either body. It is equally unlikely that an individual will seek an order from the Courts obliging the Duke to summon the Convocation and the Court would grant such an order. Although if such a case were mounted it would be a fascinating hearing.

Chapter 4

Right to take sea-sand from Cornwall's Beaches

Introduction

Some time ago I received a phone call from the Devon and Cornwall Police. They had received a complaint because someone was driving onto a beach in North Cornwall with a JCB and removing large amounts of sand. When the police challenged the individual they claimed they had a right so to do. I was asked whether such a right existed and if so what limitations if any applied? This is a matter of some controversy; there have been a number of court cases in which individuals have been accused of stealing sand from beaches. Their defence has been to claim the right to take the sand.[84] Hopefully this chapter will answer some of the questions which arise.

Background

In a Charter of Henry III dated 18 June 1261[85] it is recited a grant was made by Henry's brother Richard, Earl of Cornwall to the inhabitants of Cornwall of the right to take sand from the sea shore for the fertilization of their lands. King Henry's Charter ratified and approved his brother's grant. (See Appendix III). By the Sea Sand (Devon and Cornwall) Act 1609[86] the right was enacted in Statute. Note that the Act

---

84 See http://news.bbc.co.uk/hi/England/2680421.stm "Farmer stole sand from beach"; see also http://newsvote.bbc.co.uk/mpapps/pagetools/print/news.bbc.co.uk/1/hi/england/cornwall "Row over sand removal by farmers"

85 Charter Roll, 45 Henry III No 11, Calendar of Charter Rolls 1257-1300 p.36

86 Act 7 Jac. I c.18

extends to Devon. The 1609 Act was confirmed in subsequent legislation.[87] (See Appendix III)

The preamble to the 1609 Act provided that sea-sand had been found to be very profitable for the:

> "bettering of land and especially for the increase of corn and tillage in Devon and Cornwall, where the most part of the inhabitants had not commonly used any other "worth" for the bettering of their arable grounds and pastures, and that divers persons having lands adjoining the sea-shore had of late interrupted the bargemen and such others as had used their free wills and pleasures to fetch sea-sand from below high-water mark unless they made composition at rates fixed by those having land adjoining the shore."

The Act then provides at section 1 that it shall be lawful for all persons resident and dwelling in Devon and Cornwall to fetch and take sea-sand at all places below high-water mark where it is cast by the sea for the bettering of their land and the increase of corn and tillage at their wills and pleasures.

Section 2 than enacts that bargemen and boatmen and all other carriers of sea-sand may land sand at places where they had done so within the previous 50 years and to use such ways as had been used during the previous 20 years paying the accustomed dues.

Does the right still exist?

Frankly it is difficult to say whether the right still does exist. If it does it is clear that the right exists only for the improvement of agricultural land. That means land used for the production of food. So taking sea-sand for the purposes of an equine centre, for example, would not come with the legislation.

87 3 Car I c 5 (1627) and 16 Car I c 4 (both now repealed)

The next issue is the registration of the right under the Commons Registration Act 1965. It is a rule of law that there cannot be a right in common in a fluctuating body such as the inhabitants of a particular district.[88] There are, however, exceptions to this rule one being the grant by the Crown to the inhabitants of a district may be held to have incorporated those to whom it is made for the purposes of enjoying the benefit.[89] In a decision dated 25 January 1978 the Chief Commons Commissioner decided that:

> "any right derived from the grant or the Act of 1609, if it is a right in common, has ceased to be exercisable by virtue of section 1(2) (b) of the Act of 1965 though not having been registered."[90]

For the right to be exercisable it requires registration would appear to be confirmed in Halsbury's Laws of England.[91]

Conclusion

The right to take sand clearly did exist. Initially it applied to Cornwall and then at some point became extended to Devon. It would appear, however, that because of lack of registration under the 1965 Act it is no longer capable of being exercised. However people continue to exercise the right so maybe it continues by default. It is clear that it is a subject of much confusion and the issue are not fully understood within Devon and Cornwall generally or by the Courts in particular.

---

88 *Gateward's Case* (1607) (6 Co Rep 59b) (All ER Rep 48)

89 *Chilton v Corporation of Land* (1878) (7 Ch. D 735, 741)

90 Commons Registration Act 1965 *In the Matter of Gunwalloe Church Cove Beach, Gunwalloe, Cornwall (No. 2)* (1978) Reference No. 206/D/480

91 Halsbury's Laws of England Volume 13 (2009) 5th Edition 2. Rights of Common and Related Rights para. 465

Chapter 5

Property Rights of the Duchy of Cornwall within Cornwall and the Isles of Scilly

"This is one of the traditional things we have inherited."[92]

Introduction

The Duchy of Cornwall was established by a Charter dated 17 March 1337 which was supplemented by subsequent Charters. (These are set out in Appendix IV) It is, apparently, a quaint feudal remnant from a time long past. It was, and is, more than an estate of property and investments, such as the Duchies of Westminster or Devonshire. Until the passing of the Stannary Court (Abolition) Act 1896 it was responsible for the Stannary Courts—a judicial system which, as we have seen, at one time operated a criminal jurisdiction and included its own prisons. It had and, at least theoretically still has, the right to summon Parliaments (the Convocation of Tinners of Cornwall and the Great Court of Devon Tinners). It operated a system of taxation called coinage until its abolition in 1838.[93] In 1858 the Duchy claimed it had been granted the "territory and government of Cornwall" and the Duke had been "quasi Sovereign" of Cornwall.[94]

---

92 Statement made by Sir Walter Ross, Secretary and Keeper of the Records to Parliamentary Accounts Committee 7th February 2005 in relation to *Bona Vacantia*

93 Coinage Abolition Act 1838

94 The Tidal Estuaries, Foreshores and Under-Sea Minerals within and around

42

Today the Duchy states that it is a "well-managed private estate"[95], without any qualification to that statement. The expression is not surrounded by inverted commas to indicate some special or particular significance. This implies we are to attach to the phrase "well-managed private estate" its ordinary meaning. That cannot be correct. No private estate, well-managed or otherwise, would benefit from the privileges enjoyed by the Duchy of Cornwall.

The Duchy once enjoyed an impressive array of Royal Prerogatives which to the modern ear sounds archaic: the right of "prisage of wine"[96], the right of "great customs of wools, wool-fels and leather"[97] and the right to "seize and confiscate enemies' ships in times of war". A surprising number of other ancient rights have survived and are still exercised by the Duchy. It is these which will now be considered.

"The Duchy is not Cornwall and Cornwall is not the Duchy"[98]

The famous Cornishman, A. L. Rowse, sought to correct what he regarded as a common misconception when he wrote:

"It is first necessary to clear out of the way the popular confusion between the Duchy and the County of Cornwall. They are, of course, two entirely separate entities, utterly different in character..."[99]

---

the Coast of the County of Cornwall—Arbitration by Judge Sir John Patteson (1855)

95 www.duchyofcornwall.org/faq/htm
96 The presage of wine meant the Duke of Cornwall was entitled to one tun of wine from ships of less than 20 tons and two tuns from large ships.
97 The Duchy enjoyed the profits of port which included "Cocket" which was a custom levied on wools, woolfells and hides
98 Gill, C., "Introduction" in Gill, C., (Ed.) *The Duchy of Cornwall* (1987) p 14
99 Rowse, A. L., *West Country Stories* (1945) p 94

It is explained by the Duchy with reference to Cornwall: "the Duchy has a special relationship with the County".[100] The Law Commissioners, in relation to its report on Land Registration, which led to the Land Registration Act 2002, said:

> "Due to the complex and arcane nature of the law that governs the land holding of the Crown and the Royal Duchies of Cornwall and Lancaster; the preparation of the relevant provisions of the Bill proved to be particularly difficult."[101]

The purpose in this section is to disperse some of the "popular confusion", to explain one aspect the special relationship the Duchy has with Cornwall and to unravel some of the complex and arcane land law relating the Duchy of Cornwall. It will be demonstrated in one respect at least the "Duchy is Cornwall".

To aid understanding it is essential that some legal theory is set out and in that regard we might usefully start with Joseph Chitty who explained:

> "That the King is the universal lord and original proprietor of all lands in his kingdom; and that no man doth or can possess any part of it, but what has mediately or immediately been derived as a gift from him, to be held upon feudal services."[102]

The reference by Chitty to feudal service is valuable because to understand the system of land law within England and Wales we must reach back to a time, long past, when people acquired rights in land usually in exchange for services. It

---

100 www.duchyofcornwall.org/abouttheduchy_history_acquisition.htm
101 Law Commission and HM Land Registry Land Registration for 21st Century: A Conveyancing Revolution, Law Com 271 2001 p 243
102 Chitty, J., *A Treatise on The Law of the Prerogatives of the Crown* (1820) p 211

might be the provision of horses or salmon or the financing of men at arms in times of strife. Thus land in England and Wales is held by the landowner for a "legal estate" in fee simple.[103] The first and important point is that the landowner *does not own the land he or she owns an interest in the land* or as lawyers explain it a "legal estate". The only exception is land held by the Crown in demesne, for "no subject can hold lands allodially".[104] Allodial land describes land which is owned absolutely rather than land held of a superior lord or Sovereign. Demesne lands, in this context, are those held by the Crown as Sovereign or Lord Paramount. The ordinary meaning of "demesne" is land belonging to a feudal lord which he retains in his own possession rather than "parcelling out to his feudal tenants".[105] In simple terms while the rest of us have an "estate in land" only the Crown can actually own land. The Crown has the power to create interests in land out of its demesne land. Indeed it is the only way a "legal estate in fee simple" or freehold estate can be created. This is called "infuedation". As a result of the Statute *Quia Emptores 1290,* which can still be found on the Statute Law Database, no other landowner has the right to create a freehold from a freehold, that is to "subinfuedate". All landowners hold land in fee directly or indirectly from the Crown.

In summary land held in demesne by the Crown have the following characteristics:

- The Crown has dominion over that land as Lord Paramount; and
- The Crown has no estate in land.[106]

---

103   In what follows extensive quotes come from the Law Commission and HM Land Registry Land Registration for the 21st Century: A Conveyancing Revolution Law Com 271 2001 pages 245 et seq

104   Burke, J., *Jowitt's Dictionary of English Law* (2nd ed 1977) p 89

105   E-mail correspondence with Land Registry 12 March 2009

106   Under Scottish Law it was possible to own land allodially, for example, by

The position of the Duchy of Cornwall in this hierarchy is confusing. The Duchy of Cornwall can hold demesne land, as can any lord of a manor, in the sense it is a landowner and has retained its interest in that land without granting any of it to his tenants. The Duchy, in modern usage, has a "mesne lordship" which is a landlord who has tenants while holding his land from a superior lord. This is referred to as a "Tenure" which denotes the holding of land by a tenant under his lord and is only appropriate where the feudal relation of lord and tenant exists.[107] The Duchy holds the Duchy in fee as tenant in chief of the Sovereign. The Duke of Cornwall is "a feudal tenant of the Queen like the rest of us".[108] Thus as far as the freeholders in Cornwall are concerned the Duke stands between them and the Sovereign.[109] It is one of the few cases in which the second step of the feudal pyramid survives. The Duchy of Cornwall is one of the very rare examples where "mesne lordship" can be proved and has any continuing relevance. When "tenure" exists over a number of manors, as in the case of the Duchy is was known as a "land barony" or "honour".

In support of the above analysis the Land Registry relies on the Charter of 17 March 1337 which says:

> *"habendum et tenendum eidem duci et isius et heredum suorum regum Anglie filis primogenitis et dicti ducibus in regno Anglie hereditary successuris… de nobi et heredibus nostris impperpetuum."*

---

the church. The Abolition of Feudal Tenures etc. (Scotland) Act 2000 provides that "the entire system whereby land is held by a vassal on perpetual tenure from a superior" was abolished from 28th November 2004. All land in Scotland is now allodial.

107 Halsbury's Laws of England Volume 39(2) Para. 75 Land and Interests in Land

108 E-mail correspondence with Land Registry 12 March 2009

109 E-mail correspondence with writer and Land Registry 14th January 2010

"To have and to hold to the same Duke and the eldest sons of him and Heirs Kings of England and the Dukes of the same place hereditarily to succeed in the Kingdom of England... of us and his heirs for ever."

The Land Registry claims: "To have and to hold... of us and our heirs for ever" are standard words of infuedation by which a feudal superior grants to his tenants thus, they assert, it is clear that the possessions of the Duchy are held feudally as tenant in chief of the Crown.[110]

There are those including, arguably, the Duchy who would challenge the above analysis. They claim that the Duchy holds the lands in Cornwall allodially. This point will be addressed shortly.

The 1231 Charter of Henry III granted to his brother Richard "the whole county of Cornwall"; similarly the 1307 Charter of Edward II, to Piers Gaveston, allowed for a grant in like terms. The third Duchy Charter of 3 January 1338 brought together the various provisions of the previous two Charters. Edward III provided that:

"by this Our charter have confirmed to the said duke all Our fees, with appurtenances which We have in the said county of Cornwall or which do or shall belong or appertain to Us..."[111]

In *Chasyn v Lord Sturton* (1553)[112] it was confirmed:

"the said county should be given to Edward the son as in the name of the Duchy; and that this county of

---

110   E-mail correspondence 27 March 2009
111   See Appendix IV
112   *Chasyn v Lord Sturton* (1553) (1Dyer 94a) p 205

Cornwall should always remain a duchy... without being otherwise disposed of..."

Similarly in the *Princes Case* (1606) Lord Coke said "the whole county of Cornwall should always remain as a Duchy to the eldest sons of the Kings of England..."

Baron Adams in the *Sutton Pool Case*[113] stated: "When the Prince of Wales takes he takes an estate in fee-simple..." Later in the same case Chief Baron Parker, as some indication of the complexities which arise when considering the Duchy, said:

> "It is clear, that the Crown does not take an absolute fee, but only a qualified fee, till the birth of the King's eldest son, and when there is a King's eldest son he takes a fee but only a qualified fee till he comes to the Crown or till his own death."

In other words a Duke holds only until he becomes King or, if the Duchy has reverted to the Crown for want of a Duke, the Duchy does not become absorbed in the Crown's demesne but is held in "fee" until a Duke is born.

In *The Solicitor of the Duchy of Cornwall v the Next of Kin of Thomas Canning* (1880) the assertion was made and accepted that:

> "The charters of the duchy have always been treated both by the Courts of Judicature and the legislature as having vested in the Dukes of Cornwall the whole interest and dominion of the Crown in and over the whole county of Cornwall."[114]

---

113   *The Attorney General to HRH the Prince of Wales, Duke of Cornwall v The Mayor and Commonalty of the Borough of Plymouth and others* (1754) (Wight 134) p 1208

114   *The Solicitor to the Duchy of Cornwall v Canning* (1880) (5 P.D. 114 Probate)

The Duchy acknowledges it has a "special relationship with Cornwall". It also points out only 13 per cent of the land it owns is within Cornwall which represents 2 per cent of the geographical area of the County.[115] While the percentages are no doubt accurate they do not reflect the full extent of the connection between the Duchy and Cornwall. Indeed possibly they are intended to obscure that relationship.

Nowhere is the position of the Duchy so forcefully set out as in "Foreshore Case"[116] which includes the statement:

> "the Duchy Charters are sufficient to vest in the Dukes of Cornwall not only the government of Cornwall but the entire territorial dominion in and over the county…"

Later in the same section:

> "It cannot, therefore, reasonably be doubted that this *Royal Seignory consisted of the King's demesne lands* (emphasis added), reversion, feudal services, rights and emoluments, with the prerogatives above enumerated, did, in fact, comprehend the whole territorial interest and dominion of the Crown in and over the entire County."

In reply to a question from the Government Law Officers the Duchy answered:

> "It is contended, that the Duchy in its creation was co-extensive with the County, in the sense in which that term is used: *not that its possessor was entitled to every acre of*

---

115   www.duchyofcornwall.org/faqs.htm

116   The Tidal Estuaries, Foreshores and Under-Sea Minerals within and around the Coast of the County of Cornwall.- Arbitration by Sir John Patteson (1855) Duchy Preliminary Statement p 9

land in the County, (emphasis added) but to the great seigniorial rights throughout the County, which under the circumstances, would have been vested in the Crown."

Eight years after the Foreshore Case was arbitrated the Duchy remained quite insistent in its position regarding Cornwall. For example:

"in so far as the County of Cornwall is concerned all rights previously vested in the Crown other than that of Royal jurisdiction were vested *jure ducutus* in the Royal personage whether the Sovereign or the Duke of Cornwall…"[117]

The most explicit claim made by the Duchy was set out in 1860 as follows:

"It is well known that the ultimate fees of all lands in England are vested in the Crown by reason of its prerogative in tenure and *are incapable of being transferred to a subject. But without doubt the ultimate fees of all lands within the County of Cornwall are by the express language of this 3rd Charter vested in the Duke of Cornwall* (emphasis added) and not only so but clothed with all those prerogative rights which would attach to those Fees in the hands of the Sovereign as fully as the Sovereign could have enjoyed them if (to use the language of this Charter) the Sovereign had retained the same fees in his own hands and that *non obstante prerogative.*[118] It seems difficult to support this or any other construction than that the Duke as regards these possessions was substituted for

117 TNA TS 25/1330—Treasure Trove at Luxullian Cornwall (1864)
118 Notwithstanding the prerogative

and holds them as the Representative of the Sovereign."[119]

Shortly after, in 1862, the Trustees to the Duchy stated that the decision in the Cornwall Foreshore Case established:

"His Royal Highness as the superior Lord of the soil of the entire County of Cornwall…"[120]

There are those[121] who claim that the Duchy holds the whole of Cornwall allodially; that it is the absolute owner of the land. For them this is significant and one of the issues which indicate Cornwall's unique relationship with the English state. The implication being that the Duke of Cornwall did not hold the land from the Sovereign as a vassal but owned the land independently of feudal obligations. It would not be difficult to argue from the quotes above that the Duchy adopts a similar position. In an attempt to clarify the situation particularly in light of the passing of the *Quia Emptores* in 1290 the Land Registry was asked to answer the following question:

"Assume the Duchy wished to purchase freehold property in Truro and since the Duchy holds Cornwall in fee simple would the Duchy be granting a freehold interest to itself?"

The reply was:

"I do not really know the answer as to whether it is possible to hold a freehold interest of oneself, or

119 TNA TS 27/818—Treasure Trove (1907-1932)
120 Report to Her Majesty the Queen from the Council of H.R.H. The Prince of Wales 1862
121 Angarrack, J., *Our Future is History* (2002).
     See also www.duchyofcornwall.eu/latest/

whether that is technically what the result would be. I think it is possible because if the Crown Estate acquires freehold land by purchase I do not think the existing freehold comes to an end…. In modern conditions the question has no practical consequences… and probably has not since the Tenures Abolition Act 1660…"[122]

There is no clear answer to whether or not the Duchy owns Cornwall allodially or whether the Duchy has a freehold, or interest in land, in the whole of Cornwall. If the Duchy does hold Cornwall in fee simple then it does seem to be practising subinfeudation which has not been permissible since 1290. Whatever view is taken in one sense at least it is true that "The Duchy is Cornwall" even if "Cornwall is not the Duchy". It is difficult to think of any comparable situation applying in a territory where the Queen is Sovereign. One cannot imagine, for example, the freehold in Staffordshire being granted to a subject of the Crown.

Right to the Isles of Scilly

The Duchy confidently asserts:

"The Isles of Scilly have been part of the Duchy of Cornwall since its foundation in the 14th Century."[123]

The claim is supported by Government. For example in a letter dated 16 June 2009 from the Department of Communities and Local Government it was claimed:

"the Isles of Scilly, including St Mary's, has been part of the Duchy of Cornwall since the 14th century…"[124]

---

122 E-mail from Land Registry to writer dated 17th June 2010
123 www.duchyofcornwall.org/aroundtheduchy_islesofscilly.htm
124 Letter from Iain Wright M.P., Dept of Communities and Local Government

Despite the assurance demonstrated in the statements quoted and the public functions performed by the Duchy there is some ambiguity in the Duchy's claim to the Islands. For example, in the papers relating to the Cornwall Foreshore Case the Duchy observed:

> "These Islands, as before mentioned, were parcel of the Earldom, and held as of the Great Honor of Dunheved or Launceston; but although parcel of the Earldom, they are not expressly named in the Duchy Charter; but that the Seignory of these Islands did pass to the Dukes, though not specifically named in the Charter is clear from the *Inquisition Post Mortem* of Ranulph de Blanchminster, in the 22nd Edward III, eleven years only after the creation of the Duchy, which states that he held of the King no land in Cornwall, but that he held of the Lord Edward Duke of Cornwall the Castle of Sully with the Islands to the said Castle appertaining; and his heir being under age, the profits in the next year are accounted to the Duke."

As further evidence the Duchy cited an "Inrolment" of the Duchy of Cornwall of 22 June 1637 by which the Scilly Isles were leased to Sir William Godolphin.

There are, however, those who have raised questions about the status of the Isles of Scilly. For example, Robert Heath in his 1750 study of the Scilly Isles:

> "After the Dissolution of Abbies and monastical Estates, the ecclesiastical Jurisdiction of Scilly devolving to the See of Exeter, the Civil Power was granted by the Crown to Lords Proprietors, on Condition of their paying certain Rents into the Hands of the Receiver for

the Dutchy of Cornwall, for the Tenure of those Islands; by which they came to be acknowledg'd as Part of the Jurisdiction of the said Dutchy; but only by the King's Favour: For I cannot find by any Records that they were ever annex'd thereunto.

And here I shall observe, that in the Grant of the Dutchy of Cornwall (which I have seen) to the Prince of Wales, as eldest son of England, there is no mention made of the Islands of Scilly… whence if Scilly appertains, or is part of the said Duchy, *it is rather permitted by Favour than given to be so by Royal Authority;* especially as the Grant of those Islands to several late Proprietors, is expressed in so ample a Manner."[125] (Emphasis added)

Later in 1824 Fortescue Hitchins wrote:

"When the county of Cornwall was erected into a Duchy, these islands seem either to have been forgotten or purposely omitted as they are not mentioned in the general grant. This omission has given rise to some disputes whether they belong to the Duchy or not. It is certain that some Kings of England have made separate grants of them when there have been Dukes of Cornwall; and when the dissolution of religious houses took place, the lands which belonged to the abbey of Tavistock fell to the Crown; and hence it is presumed, that the dominion of these islands accompanied their destiny. *If, therefore Scilly is now considered as a part of the Duchy, it is rather permitted by favour, than given so by royal authority.*"[126] (Emphasis added)

---

125 Heath, Robert, *The Isles of Scilly (A natural and historical account of the Islands of Scilly)* (First published 1750)

126 Hitchins, Fortescue, *The History of Cornwall* (1824) Volume II page 687

"The following lengthy quote appeared in a memo written by a Mr. J Hall in 1889, quoting from a work of 1831, in connection with the proposed Local Government Bill:

> "It has been questioned whether (the Scilly Islands) ever belonged to the Duchy of Cornwall, as they are not specified in the grant (of the Duchy of Cornwall 17th March 1337) for the erection of the Duchy; and though it may be inferred that they were in some respects dependent on it, *there are no records to show that they were ever annexed to it.* After having been granted away by Henry VIII they reverted to the Crown by exchange, in the reign of Queen Mary; and Elizabeth, in 1571, gave them to Francis Godolphin, but after having been more than 200 years under the sway of the Godolphin's and Osbornes, Dukes of Leeds, they have again lapsed to the Crown (1831) and are at present under the Duchy of Cornwall"[126a] (Emphasis added)

"The most significant challenge to the Duchy's claim to the Scilly Isles came in 1832/1834 when the case was examined by the Law Officers of the Crown. Initially in 1832 the question was raised "as to whether the Scilly Islands formed part of the Land Revenues of the Crown…" The question was submitted to Solicitors of the Office of Woods and Forests who in two opinions dated 8th and 10th June 1832 advised the Scilly Isles belonged to the Crown.[126b] Further information was supplied which caused the solicitor to modify his opinion and

126a TNA HLG 8/75 – The Scilly Isles: Constitution and government quoting from Gorton, J. G., *A Topographical Dictionary of Great Britain and Ireland (1831-33)* Vol. III p 340
126b TNA BT 297/556 – St Mary's Pier. Scilly Isles: Mr Dorrien Smith and Duchy of Cornwall (1889-1922)

an application was made to the Law Officers of the Crown (whose opinion appears in the Appendix) who having:

> "carefully examined the origin of several documents submitted to us together with the very able statements and arguments and elaborate searches which accompany them and we are of the opinion upon the whole that the Scilly Islands are to be considered as part of the properties of the Duchy of Cornwall and they do not belong to the Crown *jura coronae*…"[127]

They also said:

> "it is to be regretted that in a matter of so much importance there should not be a regular series of authentic public documents by referring to which the question between the Crown and the Duchy of Cornwall might be at once satisfactorily decided."[128]

They went on to say:

> "we are further of the opinion under all the circumstance that there is nothing of sufficient ground to call in question the right of the Duchy as it has been asserted… *for forty years*" (Emphasis added)

The papers do not reveal why the question was raised neither do they provide copies of the documents submitted. But it is clear from the evidence that is available there is not an overwhelming unequivocal support for the Duchy's claim to the Islands. The two initial opinions found the Islands were property of the Crown and although the Law Officers later

127 Right of the Crown
128 TNA CRES 58/742—Scilly Islands (1832—1892)

took a different view they could find support only for the assertion that the Duchy had enjoyed the Islands for forty years and no since the fourteenth century as the Duchy claims. Needless to say the Law Officers opinion has never been tested in Court.

Mary Coates, in her paper to the Royal Historical Society in 1927, offers a different explanation of how the Scilly Isles became part of the Duchy:

> "*Annexata Maneria* added to the Duchy by subsequent Acts of Parliament… these included… fifteen manors confiscated by Henry VIII after attainder of Henry Courtenay, Marquis of Exeter… and lastly fifteen more obtained by the Crown through the dissolution of the Priories of Launceston and Tywardreth… in the list of the 15 Courtenay Manors we find… and the farm of the Scilly Isles."[129]

The right to the Isles of Scilly is claimed by the Duchy relying to some degree on documents which predate the Duchy Charter of 1337. They argue that they "succeeded" to the property rights and privileges of the Earls of Cornwall and thus, by implication, enjoyed the benefits of the Earldom. That argument was not accepted by the Crown in, for example, a dispute with regard to Royal Mines[129a] within Cornwall[129b] and I can find no reason to see why it should be accepted with regard to the Isles of Scilly.

---

129 Coate, Mary, "The Duchy of Cornwall: Its History and Administration 1640 to 1660" (1927) *Transactions of the Royal Historical Society* p 147

129a The right to gold and silver recovered from mines is usually a Royal Prerogative

129b TNA CRES 34/21 – Wheal Newton Question between Crown and Duchy of Cornwall as to right of Royal Mines within duchy (1859 – 1861)

What is clear is that the Crown felt able to dispose of the Islands as it wished well after the fourteenth century. Since there is no indisputable document by which it can be demonstrated the Islands were passed to the Duchy of Cornwall the questions which remain are: by what means did the Islands become the property of the Duchy and when did that take place?

Right to foreshore of Cornwall, fundus and mines and minerals under the foreshore and fundus of the riverbed.

The Duchy has a right to the foreshore and undersea minerals of Cornwall, except when they are owned by a subject, as a consequence of the Cornwall Foreshore Case and the resulting Cornwall Submarine Act 1858.

Specifically the Duke of Cornwall, in right of the Duchy of Cornwall, has the right of all mines and minerals lying under the seashore between high and lower water marks within the County of Cornwall and under estuaries and tidal rivers and other places (below low water mark) being part of the county.[130]

The Duchy also owns the "fundus" or navigable river bed and foreshore of the Tamar, Camel, Helford, Fal, and Fowey together with what are known collectively as the Devon Waters being the Salcombe and Kingsbridge Estuaries, the River Dart and the River Avon. Therefore, since the pillars of the Tamar Bridges are located on Duchy property, a modest rent was negotiated by Brunel of £25 per annum.[131] It also means, for example, part of the toll paid by those catching the ferry from Plymouth to Torpoint and King Harry's Ferry near Feock goes to the Duchy.

---

130 Halsbury's Laws of England Volume 12(1) Crown Property 3 Foreshore and Wreck para.268

131 Burnett, D., *A Royal Duchy* (1996) p 37

Right to search for and work mines in Accessionable Manors[132]

There were originally seventeen Accessionable Manors belonging to the Duchy, six of which were sold for redemption of land tax in 1798. In these certain tenements (known as "conventionary tenements") were held by way of leases. The custom that possession of the minerals was in the tenant did not apply and, therefore, the Duke of Cornwall and his licensees were entitled to get the minerals without the consent of the tenant. The Duchy of Cornwall (No. 2) Act 1844 provides a code for the working of the minerals.

Halsbury's Laws described the right as follows:

> "Subject to certain restrictions… the Duke of Cornwall and his lessees and persons authorised by him and their agents or workmen may enter land comprised in any of certain accessionable manors in which any mines, minerals, stone or substrata belong to the Duke and search dig for, open and work mines.… In so far as it is necessary or convenient for working those mines… may erect buildings, steam and other engines, machinery and things, sink and make pits, shafts, levels, adits, air holes, tram and other roads and other works… and do other acts and things upon, under, in and about land. The surface owner is *compelled* (emphasis added) to permit his land to bear these burdens and to be used for these purposes although he is not divested of his title in favour of the Duke."

The Duchy has recently caused some consternation in certain areas of Cornwall by registering its mining rights. The registration has been necessary because of a Land Registry

---

132 Halsbury's Laws of England Volume 12(1)—Casual Revenues Minerals paras. 225/226

requirement and because valuable metals have recently been discovered in Cornwall such as iridium and tungsten[133] and the Duchy wishes to protect its interests.[134]

Right to Mines Royal?

By prerogative right the Crown is entitled to all mines of gold and silver within the realm regardless of whether the mines are located on Crown land or on the land of a subject.[135] Even if a subject were to be granted lands with all mines in them Mines Royal would be excluded.[136] The Crown Estate website was unambiguous:

> "Today, the prerogative right to gold and silver are part of the Crown Estate. This is true for all of the UK although in the past, in some limited areas in Scotland, this right has been transferred from the Crown by ancient charter."[137]

Since enquiries under the Freedom of Information Act 2000 were made of the Crown Estate the website has been changed and the above statement is no longer included.

A dispute arising in the nineteenth century between the Duchy who claimed the right to Mines Royal in Cornwall and the predecessors to the Crown Estate, the Commissioners of Woods, Forest and Land Revenues matter remains unresolved: the Duchy claims Mines Royal, as confirmed in correspondence with the Attorney General to H.R.H. the Prince of

---

133 See *Times* "Australians want Cornish mines to rise again" 26th March 2012. It seems Tungsten is a "geological bedfellow of tin"

134 See *Western Morning News* "Duchy quells fears of mining under homes" 13th February 2012

135 *Case of Mines* (1567) (1 Plowd 310 at 315-316 Ex Ch.)

136 Crown Estate File 64-00-11 28 January 1988

137 www.thecrownestate.co.uk/our_portfolio/rural/minerals.htm

Wales,[138] and the Crown Estate persists in its denial of such claims. The Crown Estate continues to rely on the opinion of the Law Officers dated 29 May 1860 (see Appendix V) in which they state:

"Royal Mines are a prerogative of so high a character as not to pass by any royal grant except by express words of which we find none…"[139]

The Royal Mines Acts of 1688 and 1693 provided essentially if gold or silver were a by product of mining for tin, copper, iron or lead (with certain saving provisions to protect the Stannaries) the subject could continue to enjoy the mine. The Acts do not make special provision for the Duchy of Cornwall.

The matter was raised by the solicitor to the Duchy on 16 June 1980.[140] No new evidence was provided and the Crown Estate maintained its position. It insists "that it is for the Duchy to establish as against the Crown, its right to Mines Royal".[141] The Crown Estate had, for many years, been granting licenses to various companies to prospect for gold and silver within Cornwall without reference to the Duchy. Indeed it said they saw "no reason why the (Duchy) should be informed".[142] A provision of the Limitation Act 1980 section 37(6) was noted, however. As observed by the Crown Estate this says:

"Nothing in this Act shall affect the prerogative right of Her Majesty (whether in right of the Crown or of the

---

138   Letter to writer from Mr Jonathan Crow, Q.C. Attorney General to H.R.H. the Prince of Wales 24th October 2011

139   TNA T 1/16350—Duchy of Cornwall: arbitration on Crown's right to royal gold and silver mines in Cornwall (1879) and TNA T 1/12673—Duchy of Cornwall—question of title to Royal Mines to be settled by arbitration (1880)

140   Crown Estate File 64-00-11

141   Crown Estate Memo 2 February 1988 J Stumbke Legal Adviser

142   Crown Estate Memo 3rd February 1988 M L Davies Legal Adviser

Duchy of Lancaster) or of the Duke of Cornwall to any gold or silver mine."[143]

A Legal Adviser to the Crown Estate gave his opinion that the section was not decisive "about the existence Mines Royal rights in the Duke of Cornwall... (It is) however a statutory sign-post to the possible existence of such rights."[144] In the same memo he said "The Duchy's protective efforts go back a long way". In 1996 the Duchy solicitors wrote to the Crown Estate advising they had been instructed by the Duchy to agree that the Crown Estate:

"continue to authorise prospecting licenses throughout the country, including Cornwall without prejudice to the Duchy's claim.

If workable deposits are discovered, then the Duchy reserves its full rights in relation to them and would expect to grant an operating license."[145]

In September 2000 Guinness, then the sponsors of Six Nations Rugby, intended to commission a trophy to be made from gold from England, France, Ireland, Italy, Scotland and Wales. The English gold was to come from Hope's Nose in Cornwall. The question was how was legal title to be obtained for the English gold.[146] The enquiry was not passed to the Duchy, "so far as it relates to Cornish gold... which might imply that we recognize that they have exclusive rights."[147] The delay in getting a

143 Limitation Act 1980
144 Crown Estate File 64 00 13 Memo 30th September 1996
145 Letter from Farrer & Co 20 September 1996 to Crown Estate Office
146 Letter Wardell Armstrong Crown Mineral Agent 15 September 2000 to Crown Estate.
147 Crown Estate Memo 3 October 2000 File Number 64 00 13 D Harris Legal Adviser

response was such that sadly the issue was never pursued and the proposed trophy was not produced.

The matter rests with both sides maintaining their positions. The Duchy claims Mines Royal in Cornwall and the Crown Estate rejects the claim. However, one can be sure if a Mine Royal were to be developed in Cornwall then the issue would be vigorously pursued by both sides. After more than one hundred and fifty years neither the Crown nor the Duchy appears ready to concede.

Right to Escheat

This right is described in Joseph Chitty as:

> "the last fruit or incident resulting from the feudal system. It was a species of confiscation by which the feu reverted to the Sovereign…"[148]

Escheat is the capacity of the chief lord to resume land granted by him or a predecessor in title on determination of the estate granted. It applies only when a freehold estate determines. In Cornwall it passes to the Duchy by virtue of the Duchy's estate in fee simple. The lord to whom the land reverts completes the escheat only when he takes possession or control of it or takes proceedings for its recovery. The circumstances in which escheat occurs are as follows:

1   where freehold land is disclaimed in cases that normally involve insolvency as when a trustee in bankruptcy disclaims onerous property under Insolvency Act 1986 section 315 or a liquidator of a company disclaims under section 178 of the Insolvency Act 1986;

2   where under Companies Act 1985 section 654 a company is dissolved and the property is disclaimed. This

---

148   Chitty, J., *A Treatise on the Law of the Prerogatives of the Crown* (1820) p 213

is the most common reason for escheat. (The address of the Registered Office of the Company determines whether the matter is dealt with by the Duchy of Cornwall or Lancaster or the Treasury Solicitor.); and

3 Escheat can also arise on dissolution of a foreign company, or an Industrial and Provident Society ceasing to exist or on dissolution of a statutory company.[149]

The position as set out above is based on the Law Commission Report 2001 and advice provided by the Land Registry which said:

"The Duke's right to escheat in respect of land in Cornwall is not in doubt (see e.g. *Re Canning, Solicitor to the Duchy of Cornwall v Canning* (1880) (5 PD 114)"[150]

However the solicitor, Mr. Boyd-Carpenter, to the Duchy of Cornwall raised some doubts whether that analysis is correct. In a letter to the Crown Estate Office in February 1988 he wrote[151]:

"The original Charter of 1337 granted to the Dukes of Cornwall a number of specific manors, particularly in Cornwall but also elsewhere in the Country, together with various rights, including "Wards Reliefs Escheats and services of Tenants". The precise significance is a little unclear. It could either mean that the Duchy was simply being granted normal Escheats within each manor… or it could have wider significance. The wider

149 See Law Commission and HM Land Registry Land Registration in the 21st Century: A Coveyancing Revolution, Law Com 271 (2001) page 252 for a fuller explanation
150 E-mail to writer from Land Registry 14th January 2010
151 Letter solicitor to the Duchy of Cornwall M. H. Boyd-Carpenter to Crown Estate Office 24th February 1988

significance is not unconnected with the general scope and nature of the Duchy's rights in Cornwall and elsewhere…"

It is claimed that the Duchy's right of escheat included the honours of Trematon, Launceston and Bradninch only.[152] Chynoweth points out during the Tudor period both the Crown and the Duchy appointed escheators for Cornwall. The Duchy's escheator enquired into lands which were reputed to be held of itself.[153] This would confirm the doubt raised in the letter from the Duchy's solicitor.

As a result of considerable confusion in the seventeenth century when the Crown attempted to revive its feudal revenues:

"it appears that an agreement was reached between the parties in 1620… (The agreement) (See Appendix VI) does not deal specifically with escheats but was taken to extend to escheats.

The result of the agreement is that in return for the Duchy conceding feudal rights in the country elsewhere, the Crown conceded the Duchy's feudal rights throughout Cornwall."

In conclusion Mr. Boyd Carpenter suggested:

"The present position, therefore, is somewhat unsatisfactory, and I think it would be sensible to resolve it by agreement.

It would therefore probably be sensible to confirm the (1620) Agreement, and we could at the same time

---

152 Clowes, R. L., "Escheators of Devon and Cornwall" (1930-31) *Devon and Cornwall Notes and Queries* Volume XVI p 201
153 Chynoweth, J., *Tudor Cornwall* (2002) p 202

define the boundary. In general terms, I believe that the boundary of Cornwall in 1337 and in 1620 was the same as it is now… it may be sensible to expressly to confirm that Cornwall includes the Isles of Scilly."

The matter came up for discussion again in 1998 in correspondence between the Crown Estate and Farrer & Co, solicitors to the Duchy of Cornwall. In a letter Farrer & Co said in relation to the 1620 Agreement:

"I have some doubts as to whether the Articles of Agreement are legally binding because the Duchy had no power to dispose of lands or interests in land before 1844 except under specific parliamentary authority. Nevertheless these have now stood for many years and I think it sensible to operate on the basis that the Agreement of 1620 still operates."[154]

The Crown Estate in a response dated 5 June 1998 pointed out the Agreement of 1620 made no mention of escheats to which Farrer & Co responded by saying:

"I have considerable doubt whether the terms of the Articles of Agreement could under the Duchy Charter be made binding on subsequent Dukes…"[155]

The Duchy would appear to have acquired a right to which it was not originally entitled. The matter is now covered by Statute.

In summary if escheat arises within the rest of England then that estate in land would cease and the land will fall to the Crown in demesne. If, however, the freehold property is in

154 Letter 13 May 1998 from Farrer & Co to Crown Estate
155 Letter dated 10 June 1998 from Farrer & Co to Crown Estate

Cornwall and escheat arises then that estate in land would become submerged in the "fee" owned by the Duchy of Cornwall as "mesne" lord.

Right to bona vacantia

The term *bona vacantia* is now applied to the estate of persons dying wholly or partially intestate and without persons within the statutory classes. In simple terms there are no legal heirs. The legal basis and effect of the transfer of the Crown's *bona vacantia* function to the Duchy is illustrated by the Privy Council's analysis of the similar transfer of function involving the Duchy of Lancaster in *Dyke v Walford* (1846).[156] It also applies to property and rights of a dissolved company and certain other corporations and, finally, certain other interests including certain interests in trust property.[157]

Bona vacantia is vested in the Crown either as monarch or as Duke of Lancaster. However within Cornwall *bona vacantia* vests in the Duke of Cornwall or the Duchy if there is no Duke.[158]

Mr. Ross, as he then was, Secretary and Keeper of the Records of the Duchy of Cornwall, when appearing before the Public Accounts Committee of the House of Commons on 7 February 2005[159] on behalf the Duchy in answer to a question regarding *bona vacantia* stated:

"This is one of the traditional things we have inherited."

The money vested in the Duchy by right of *bona vacantia* for the year ending the 31st of March 2012 was £552,000[160] (2011

---

156 *Dyke v Walford* (1846) (5 Moo PCC 434 at 495)
157 Halsbury's Laws of England Volume 12(1) Crown Property/Casual Revenue para. 235
158 Administration of Estates Act 1925 section 46/Companies Act 1925 section 1012
159 House of Commons Public Accounts Committee 7th February 2005
160 Duchy of Cornwall Accounts 31st March 2012

£75,000)[161] is, after various deductions, placed in the Duke of Cornwall's Benevolent Fund, a registered charity. Mr. Ross explained:

> "It is a charity. It is used for education religion etc. We try to focus it back into the area from which it has come."

The Duchy of Cornwall website states the money is used in the South West. Since the funds all come from Cornwall you would expect it all to be spent in Cornwall. A large part is, but not all.

To summarize: the estate of someone who dies in Somerset without a will and without statutory heirs would pass to the Crown. However, if a similar situation arose in Cornwall it would pass to the Duchy of Cornwall.

Right to Royal Fish

Royal fish were one of the casual revenues reserved to the Crown by the statute *De Prærogativa Regis* 1324.[162] The right applies to fish taken in the seas forming "parcel" of the Crown's or Duchy's dominions. If taken in the wide seas they belong to the taker.[163] On the capture of a whale "in the narrow seas adjoining the coast, being a royal fish, the head belongs to the King while the tail belongs to the Queen";[164] presumably in the case of the Duchy of Cornwall between the Duke and Duchess. Blackstone wrote that "the reason for this whimsical division, as assigned by our ancient records, was to furnish the Queen's wardrobe with whalebone. The reason is more whimsical than the division, for the whalebone lies entirely in

---

161   Rayner, Gordon "£1 million for those without wills passes to Prince Charles' estate" *Telegraph* 3rd October 2012
162   Karraker, Cyrus H., "Royal Fish" (1936) *Quarterly Review Vol 267 pp 129-136*
163   Halsbury's Laws of England Volume 12(1) 229 *Crown Property Casual Revenues Royal Fish*
164   Halsbury's Laws of England vol. 8, para. 959

the head."[165] Whale oil, of course, was valuable as was the blubber and meat. Porpoises, grampuses and sturgeons were regarded as great delicacies.

The right was once valuable. Today it is likely to be costly since the Duchy has the obligation to remove any such Royal Fish washed up on a foreshore for which it is responsible. As an illustration of this a whale was recently washed up on the North Cornwall coast. The Marine Coastguard Agency advised that it can cost as much as £50,000 to remove since a whale now represents a health hazard containing as they do all sorts of toxic chemicals.[166]

Right to wrecks

This was a right which the Duchy decided to reassert during the nineteenth century after allowing it to lapse for some time because some: "small revenue may now therefore be anticipated from this source without material expense to the Duchy."[167]

The full extent of this right has been the topic of considerable correspondence between Government and the Duchy. There is one file in the National Archive which is thick with papers dating from 1856 to 1985.[168] For a wreck to be a wreck, until recently, it must form part of a ship[169] and must come to land.[170] It did not comprise "droits of Admiralty" which included flotsam, (goods lost from a ship which has sunk or

---

165 Blackstone, Sir William, *Commentaries on the laws of England Volume 1* (1832) p 169 et seq

166 See for example Law, R.R., et al *Metals and organochlorines in tissues of a Blainville's beaked whale (Mesoplodan densirostris) and a killer whale (Orcinus orca) stranded in the United Kingdom* (1997) Marine Pollution Bulletin 34:208

167 Report to H.M. The Queen from the Council of H.R.H. Prince of Wales (1862) p 15

168 TNA BT 243/262—The Duchy of Cornwall: Legislation relating to right of wreck of the sea (1856—1985)

169 Merchant Shipping Act 1995

170 *Sir Henry Constables Case* (1601) (5 Co Rep 106a)

perished but which have floated), jetsam, (goods cast overboard to lighten a vessel) and lagan, (goods cast overboard but buoyed so that they could be recovered later. The final "droit of Admiralty", derelict, property, including vessels abandoned and deserted without hope of recovery, was claimed by the Duchy as late as 1985 but was never conceded by the Government.[171] The point is now mute since the definition of wreck includes the "droits of Admiralty."[172]

Right to Treasure Trove

The rules regarding treasure trove traditionally provided that any gold or silver in coin, plate or bullion found deliberately concealed in a house or in earth or other private place with the intention of recover, the owner thereof being unknown, belonged to the Crown or a grantee having franchise of treasure trove. The Treasure Act 1996 replaces the old provisions. Treasure found in whatever the circumstances in which it was left vests in the franchisee, if there is one, or the Crown.[173] Within Cornwall the right to Treasure Trove belongs to the Duchy unless there is a franchisee.[174]

Right to "present clerical livings"

The possessor of the Duchy holds advowson, which is has the right to present a nominee to certain parishes of the Church of England when a vacancy arises. This is a property right (an "incorporeal hereditament"). The Duke of Cornwall makes representations to the relevant Bishop in relation to any choice. The Bishop has to agree any appointment.

---

171 TNA BT 243/262—The Duchy of Cornwall: Legislation relating to right of wreck of the sea (1856-1985)
172 Merchant Shipping Repeal Act 1854 section 10
173 Halsbury's Laws of England Volume 12(1) Crown Chattels and Personalty para. 373
174 Halsbury's Encyclopedia of Forms and Precedents vol. 29 para. 104. See also TNA TS 25/1330 Treasure at Luxulian (1864)

The relevant parishes are: Calstock, Lanteglos by Camelford, Stoke Climsland, the Isles of Scilly, St. Domic, Landulph and St. Mellion with Pillaton (joint patron), St Buryan, St. Levan and Sennen, St. Tudy with St. Mabyn and Michaelstow (joint patron), Stratton and Launcells, Egloskerry, North Petherwin, Tremaine and Tresmere (joint patron), Boyton, North Tamerton, Werrington with St. Giles in the Heath and Virginstow (joint patron) and Boscastle with Davidstow (joint patron).[175]

This seemingly unremarkable privilege was the subject of a secret Cabinet Paper in 1924 entitled "Measures of the National Assembly of the Church of England".[176] It was discussed again in 1937 when a question was raised about who had the right to exercise the "Ecclesiastical Patronage of the Duchy of Cornwall" when the there was no Duke.[177]

It was concluded the Sovereign exercised the right as if he were Duke.

Conclusion

Many of the rights set out above are the source of substantial income for the Duchy. The right to the foreshore means the Duchy receives revenue from those wishing to park on certain Cornish beaches or operate surf schools and so on. It charges mooring fees on those rivers where it owns the fundus. Similarly its right to the Isles of Scilly, to the frustration of some on those Islands, is a valuable asset.

The right to *bona vacantia* and escheat do not arise often and the money which is raised is now largely devoted to charitable purposes. The figures are not insignificant as the over £500,000 received in 2012 demonstrates.

---

175 Mr Walter Ross, Secretary and Keeper of the Rolls 18th July 2011
176 TNA CAB 24/166—Measures of the National Assembly of the Church of England (1924)
177 TNA LO 3/1177—Ecclesiastical Patronage of the Duchy of Cornwall (1937)

There are rights which the Duchy fought to assert when they were regarded as a possible source of income, for example, the right to wreck. Now they have the potential to be an embarrassing liability and the Duchy prefers to disclaim them if it can. It is also worthy of note those claims which the Duchy makes, often with great confidence, are not as certain as might be supposed, for example, the claim to the Isles of Scilly and the right to Royal Mines.

The unique position of Cornwall in relation to the rest of the United Kingdom is nowhere better illustrated than the fact that the whole county is, depending upon your point of view, either owned allodially or is held by the Duke in fee from the Crown. Consider if the Duchy of Devonshire, a private estate, held the whole of Devon in fee and therefore enjoyed the rights arising from that situation. "The Duchy is Cornwall", despite the assertion to the contrary made by the Duchy and Government. The Duchy does not simply enjoy a special relationship with Cornwall it either owns the lands of Cornwall or holds a "legal estate" in the whole county.

Chapter 6

The Duchy of Cornwall's "Sovereign Rights" in Cornwall and the Isles of Scilly

Introduction

This chapter will be quite brief since some of the issues raised have either been explored in a previous chapter or will be examined in more detail in a later chapter. Despite the heading more general rights enjoyed by the Duchy of Cornwall are also explored so that a fuller picture is outlined.

Right to "Prick" or appoint the High Sheriff of Cornwall

It is the Duke of Cornwall and not the Crown who appoints the High Sheriff for Cornwall. This right pre-dates the Charter of 17 March 1337 which created the Duchy and dates back to the thirteenth century and the Earls of Cornwall. The position of High Sheriff is now largely ceremonial though in times past the Sheriff was an important person with considerable powers having control of the Duchy government and courts. The opening words of the oath taken by the High Sheriffs of Cornwall are:

"I XXXX do swear that I will well and truly serve as the well the Queen's Majesty as His Highness XXXX Duke of Cornwall in the office of Sheriff of the County of Cornwall and promote Her Majesty's and His Royal

Highness's profit in all things that belong to my Office
as far as I legally can or may…"[178]

Right to summon the Convocation of the Tinners of Cornwall and the Great Court of the Devon Tinners

This topic has been explored already. The Duke of Cornwall,
through the Lord Warden of the Stannaries has, at least the
theoretical right, to summon the Convocation of the Tinners
of Cornwall and the Great Court of the Devon Tinners and to
give Royal Assent to Acts passed by it.

If this right still exists it must extend to the equivalent
Convocation in Devon.

Rights applicable to the solicitor to the Duchy of Cornwall and the Attorney General to H.R.H. the Prince of Wales, Duke of Cornwall

Although this right is not specifically applicable to the Duchy's
rights in Cornwall it is of general interest. It means the
Attorney General to the Prince of Wales being a barrister or
the solicitor to the Duchy of Cornwall need not be called to
the English and Welsh Bar (if a barrister) or hold a practising
certificate (if a solicitor) although they invariably do.[179]

It is interesting it arises under the Stannaries Act 1855
Section 31 which says:

> "Whenever any person shall be appointed by his Royal
> Highness the Prince of Wales… at act as attorney or
> solicitor in the affairs of the said Duchy… it shall be
> lawful for such person to act and practice… any statute,
> order, rule, usage, or custom relating to attornies or

178 Cornwall Record Office QS 12/16/5
179 Stannaries Act 1855 Section 31, Solicitor Act 1974 Section 88 and Legal
     Services Act 2007 Section 193

solicitors, or the admission, inrolment, or practice of attornies or solicitors to the contrary notwithstanding."

The right of the Prince of Wales, Duke of Cornwall to be represented by his own Attorney General

Like the above right of general interest. It is clearly decided that the Prince of Wales, as Duke of Cornwall, does enjoy such a right which is unique for someone defined as a subject of the Crown.[180]

Right to Crown Immunity

This will be examined in the following Chapter.

Right not to pay tax[181]

Because the Duke and Duchy of Cornwall enjoy Crown Immunity they enjoy significant tax advantages. The Duke of Cornwall pays income tax on his income from the Duchy on a voluntary basis and the Duchy does not pay Capital Gains Tax. It clearly gives the Duchy a substantial economic advantage.

Right of Prince of Wales to give consent to Parliamentary Bills in relation to interests of the Duchy of Cornwall

Please see the succeeding Chapter for a full discussion of this right.

---

180 *Attorney General to H.R.H., Prince of Wales, Duke of Cornwall v Sir John St. Aubyn and others* (1811) (Wight 167)

181 See Memorandum of Understanding on Royal Taxation March 2013 pursuant Sovereign Grant Act 2011 section 5(4)

Right of the Duchy not to be extinguished for want of a Duke

There may not be a Duke but there is always a Duchy. From 1900 until 1936 there was a Duke of Cornwall. From 1936 until 1952 there was no Duke of Cornwall. There has been a Duke of Cornwall since 1952 albeit a minor until 1969. Sometimes the Duchy is in the hands of a "subject of the Crown", sometimes in the hands of the Crown.

Statutory Harbour Authority in respect of the Isles of Scilly: St Mary's Harbour

Under the Pier and Harbour Order Confirmation (No 4) Act 1890 ("the 1890 Act"), the St Mary's (Isles of Scilly) Harbour Revision Order 2007 ("the 2007 Order") which includes most of the provisions of the Harbours Docks and Piers Causes Act 1847 ("the 1847 Act") the Duchy is the Statutory Harbour Authority ("Statutory HA") for the Isles of Scilly. In this capacity the Duchy exercises a variety of public administrative functions as follows.

Under the Harbours Act 1964, as Statutory HA it has the "powers or duties of improving, maintaining or managing a harbour". This power and duty is imposed on the Duchy by virtue of the 1890 Act as expanded by the 2007 Order. As Statutory HA the Duchy is also the relevant body under the Merchant Shipping Act 1995, the Prevention of Pollution (Reception of Facilities) Order 1984, the Dangerous Vessels Act 1985, the Dangerous Substances in Harbour Areas Regulations and provisions under the Merchant Shipping and Maritime Security Act 1997 and Pilotage Act 1987

Douglas and Green on the Laws of Harbours, Coast and Pilotage[182] state the powers granted to a harbour authority are in virtually all cases "for the purpose of providing a public

---

182 Green, G K., et al—*Douglas & Green on the Laws of Harbours, Coasts and Pilotage 5th Edition*, (1997)

service". As illustrated in *Re Salisbury Railway*[183] the court interpreted section 33 of the 1847 Act as imposing the implied obligation to continue to maintain the harbour for the benefit of the public.

The Duchy has the right to deepen, dredge, scour and improve the bed and foreshore of the harbour to render it safe for traffic. Under the Merchant Shipping Act 1995 the Duchy is the local lighthouse authority under which it has power to mark and light the harbour area. It has the power to remove wrecks from the harbour area. The Harbour Master, who is appointed by the Duchy, has the capability to issue binding directions regulating the activities of ships using the harbour. In *Guelder Rose*[184] Lord Widgery C.J. said the function of the Harbour Master: "is to control and regulate (shipping) rather like a traffic policeman regulating traffic." Under the Dangerous Vessels Act 1985 the Duchy may exclude ships from the harbour if they constitute a danger to the public. Failure to comply with such a direction is a criminal offence. As Statutory HA under section 83 of the 1847 Act there is authority for the Duchy to enact bye-laws for the management of the harbour area. Under section 57 of the Criminal Justice Act 1988 breach of these bye-laws is a criminal offence punishable by fine.

The Duchy is, also, subject to a wide range of obligations concerning the environment, conservation, freedom of public access to places of natural beauty etc. It also has duties with regard to the prevention of pollution under section 144 of the Merchant Shipping Act 1995. As Statutory HA in its capacity as a marine pilotage authority, under section 1 of the Pilotage Act 1987, it has a statutory duty and power to protect public safety and the environment. The Duchy regulates, administers and licenses pilots within its harbour areas and approaches. It

183 *Re Salisbury Railway and Market House Co* (1967) (3 WLR 651)
184 *The Guelder Rose* (1927) (136 LT 226)

decides the age, fitness, experience and skills necessary to qualify as a pilot and has the obligation to suspend an authorization on grounds of incompetence, misconduct etc. The Pilotage Act 1987 imposes a wide range of additional functions and duties on the Duchy in connection with its position as Statutory HA.

All the duties set out above arise from the fact that they have been imposed by statute and are without doubt public administrative functions and the Duchy is, therefore, a public authority at least as far as the EIRs are concerned.

Conclusion

The previous and this Chapter give some indication of the rights and indeed obligations enjoyed by the Duchy and in particular how many of those are particular to its relationship with Cornwall.

Chapter 7

The Duchy of Cornwall and Parliamentary Usage

"WE ARE OF OPINION THAT the same principles which render the provisions of an Act of Parliament inapplicable to the Crown unless the Crown is expressly named, apply also to the Prince of Wales in his capacity as Duke of Cornwall."[185]

Introduction

This chapter considers "rights" enjoyed by the Duchy which have a wider application than just its relationship with Cornwall together with those advantages others do not enjoy. These rights directly impact on a number of people such as those holding leases from the Duchy of Cornwall who live on the Scilly Isles.

 The Duchy has a "right" to be consulted and give consent to legislation which affects its interests. This procedure is not a matter of constitutional nicety. A "private estate" whose head is a subject of the Crown is consulted on laws affecting its interest ("hereditary revenues, personal property or other interests").[186] It is difficult to discover how the procedure operates and what, if any, changes are made to Bills before Parliament to accommodate the requirements of that "private estate". The Duchy also enjoys the benefit of "Crown Immunity".

185 TNA LO 3/467—Duchy of Cornwall Land Tax and valuation (1913)
186 Letter from Dept. of Education to writer dated 4th August 2011

In this Chapter and the next the legal basis upon which those rights are founded will be considered as well as the advantages they offer the Duchy and Duke of Cornwall.

The Constitutional Position of the Prince of Wales, Duke of Cornwall

Prince Charles has been accused of meddling in Government policy.[187] He is quoted as saying "What some people call meddling I call mobilising."[188] It is no part of this publication to defend or attack the Prince of Wales. Suffice to say he is placed in a difficult position. Born in 1948 he has been heir to the throne since 1952 and has become the longest serving of all the Dukes of Cornwall. He is at an age when many people are thinking about retirement. If his mother enjoys longevity similar to that of his grandmother he may be waiting another decade before ascending to the throne. He is clearly concerned about the world in which he finds himself and, because of his position, is able to influence events in ways which he regards as beneficial. He has chosen the role of "seeking to make a difference—not as King but as Prince of Wales."[189]

His constitutional situation is ambiguous it: "has appeared to be rather unclear and largely unexplored."[190] The Prince has "acknowledged that there is no established constitutional role for the heir to the throne."[191] Whether deliberate or not, Prince Charles appears to have taken advantage of that ambiguity to carve out a role for himself unlike that of any of

---

187 See for example *Mail on Sunday* 3rd July 2011 article entitled "H.R.H. The Prince Minister: Charles accused of meddling after he summons seven senior Ministers to Clarence House in just ten months". See also the *Guardian* 21 August 2011 "Royal charities lobbied ministers and officials"

188 *Guardian* 21 August 2011 "Royal charities lobbied ministers and officials"

189 *Evans v Information Commissioner and Others* (2012) (UKUT 313 (AAC)) p 3

190 Brazier, R., "The constitutional position of the Prince of Wales" (1995) *Public Law* p 401

191 *Evans v Information Commissioner and Others* (2012) (UKUT 313 (AAC)) p 3

his predecessors and, possibly, create a new constitutional convention.

The legal texts are clear:

> "The Heir Apparent and his wife occupy the same legal status as private citizens apart from *the special privileges he enjoys as Duke of Cornwall.*"[192] (emphasis added)

The Courts are unambiguous:

> "the Prince of Wales, even with regard to the possessions of the Dutchy of Cornwall, was only to be considered as other subjects would be..."[193]

According to "Extracts from Shorthand Writers Notes—21st May 1817" Lord Redesdale in the House of Lords in the case of "*Sir John St Aubyn and Others... Appellants and The Attorney General of the Prince of Wales and Another... Respondents*" said:

> "That Charter (the Charter of 17th March 1337) does not according to my recollection contain a communication of Privileges or Prerogatives of the Crown or give the Prince of Wales to whom the Charter was originally granted according to the terms of the Charter any rights which did not exist in the Earls of Cornwall prior to the issuing of that Charter and nothing can be found as far as I have been able to trace the evidence on the subject to show that the Earls of Cornwall had any rights beyond those of other subjects under similar grants—*therefore looking to the Charter itself it will be extremely difficult as it seems to me to find that the Prince*

---

192   Halsbury's Laws of England Volume 12(1)/ 3 The Royal Family para. 31
193   *Attorney General to H.R.H. Prince of Wales, Duke of Cornwall v The Mayor and Commonalty of the Borough of Plymouth* (1754) (Wight 134)

of Wales as Duke of Cornwall stands in any other relation than that of a Subject considering him merely as Duke of Cornwall."[194] (emphasis added)[195]

Despite what is said above it is surely sensible for the heir to the throne to be instructed in the business of government to prepare him for kingship. This was sometimes called the "Apprenticeship Convention" although the term "Educational Convention" is now preferred.[196] What is novel, however, is Prince Charles apparently appropriating rights similar to those enjoyed by the Sovereign which are, to quote Bagehot's famous dictum:

"the right to be consulted, the right to encourage, the right to warn."[197]

While Prince Charles enjoys many splendid titles including Prince of Wales, Prince and Great (or High) Steward of Scotland,[198] Duke of Rothesay, Earl of Chester, Baron Renfrew and Lord of the Isles, it is as Duke of Cornwall and primarily as Duke of Cornwall that he has he come to enjoy constitutional privileges and benefits not available to other

---

194 TNA TS 27/818—Treasure Trove (1907—1932)

195 Although the quote comes from a document contained within the National Archive record its origin is not clear. There is no record of a case being read before the House of Lords and no reference in Hansard.

196 For an examination of the conventions with regard to the heir to the throne see *Evans v ICO and Others* (2012) (UKUT 313 (AAC))

197 Bagehot, Walter, *"The English Constitution"* Ed. Richard Crossman (1963) p 111

198 The titles Prince and Great (or High) Steward of Scotland appear to be inseparably connected. The Great (or High Steward) of Scotland is a hereditary office dating from the twelfth century. The designation "Principality of Scotland" implies not Scotland as a whole but the lands in Renfrew and the Stewartry appropriated as the patrimony of the monarch's eldest son for his maintenance. (See Office of Parliamentary Counsel—Queen's or Prince's Consent" para 47 Appendix L)

"private citizens" or "subjects of the crown". It is as the Duke of Cornwall that Prince Charles has a right to be consulted and give consent to legislation and enjoys the right to Crown Immunity.[199] So while Prince Charles may have collected unto himself, by default, various other rights it is those privileges he enjoys as Duke of Cornwall with which we shall now be concerned.

The Prince of Wales' as Duke of Cornwall's Consent[199a]

Erskine May's Treatise on the Law, Privileges, Proceedings and Usages of Parliament, 23rd Edition said:

> "Bills affecting the prerogative (being powers exercisable by the Sovereign for the performance of constitutional duties on the one hand, or, hereditary revenues, personal property or interests of the Crown, the Duchy of Lancaster or the Duchy of Cornwall on the other), require the signification of Queen's consent in both Houses before they are passed. *When the Prince of Wales is of age, his own consent as Duke of Cornwall is given.* (emphasis added)"[200]

---

199   On very rare occasions the consent as Prince and Steward of Scotland has been requested particularly in connection with changes to land and feudal law in Scotland. It is possible it has now been superseded altogether. There have also been a very few circumstances in which the consent of the Prince of Wales as Prince of Wales has been obtained (See Office of Parliamentary Counsel—Queen's or Prince's Consent" para 46 et seq. Appendix L)

199a The consent has recently been examined by the House of Commons "Political and Constitutional Reform Committee – See HC "The impact of the Queen's and Prince's Consent on the Legislative Process" HC 784 (2014)

200   Erskine May's Treatise on the Law, Privileges, Proceedings and Usage of Parliament (23rd Edition) (2004) pages 708-710.
      See also Parliamentary Counsel http://www.cabinetoffice.gov.uk/making-legislation-guide/queens_consent.aspx.
      Also e-mail from Adrian.Hitchins@parliament.uk to writer.

The 24th Edition of Erskine May[201] uses a significantly different formulation as follows:

> "The Prince's consent is required for a bill which affects the rights of the principality of Wales, the earldom of Chester or which makes specific reference or makes special provision for the Duchy of Cornwall. The Prince's consent may, depending on circumstances, be required for a bill which amends an act which does any of these things. *The need for consent arises from the sovereign's reversionary interest in the Duchy of Cornwall.*" (emphasis added)

The House of Lords Act 1999 is an example of why reference to the Principality of Wales and the Earldom of Chester were imported. Since these are, in effect, life peerages agreement had to be obtained that Prince Charles would surrender his right to sit in the House of Lords.[202] The changes, however, are viewed in some quarters with deep suspicion:

> "(the text was altered) so as to mislead the enquirer and disguise the extant constitutional position of the Duchy of Cornwall. The intention was to diminish the status of the Duchy by spuriously including the "Principality of Wales and the Earldom of Chester…"[203]

A Freedom of Information request was sent to the House of Commons asking for sight of the background papers leading to the change. The reply received was:

---

201 Erskine May's Treatise on the Law, Privileges and Usage of Parliament (24th Edition) (2011) pages 684-688

202 Jack, Sir Malcolm, (Ed.) *Erskine May—Parliamentary Practice 24th Edition* (2011) p 663

203 www.duchyofcornwall.eu/latest/

"The House of Commons does not hold copies of the papers and documents in which changes... were considered or any papers which decided a change was necessary."

They also pointed out:

"Erskine May is copyright of the May Memorial Fund Trustees, registered charity 306057. The May Memorial Trust is not a public body under the Freedom of Information Act."[204]

There is a distinction between the "assent" of the Sovereign which is necessary for all Bills before they become an "Act of Parliament" and the "consent" of the Sovereign to a Bill which affects her "hereditary revenue, personal property or other interest". In the latter case "consent" is required before a Bill can be introduced to Parliament. When consent to a Bill, which requires it, has been withheld by the Sovereign the Bill was withdrawn.[205] Where such consent by the Sovereign has been inadvertently omitted and the Bill has been read a third time, and passed, the proceedings have been declared null and void.[206] On the advice of Ministers the consent of the Sovereign is refused as a means to block the progress of a private members bill.[207]

204 E-mail to writer from Head of Information Rights and Information Security dated 28th February 2012

205 See 76 Lords Journals 478, 504; 121 Commons Journals 423; 191 Official Report (3rd series), 29 April 1868, col. 1564

206 See 107 Commons Journals 157; 166 Commons Journals 388; 204 Commons Journals 323; see also Speaker's ruling 203 HC Official Report (5th series), 1 March 1927, col. 218. On 19th November 1987 the Queen gave consent to the Felixstowe Dock and Railway Bill had been properly obtained but not notified to the House of Commons was allowed to proceed.

207 See Office of Parliamentary Counsel—"Queen's or Prince's Consent" para.132

While the consent of the Sovereign as outlined above is a matter of constitutional law the consent of the Duke of Cornwall is a matter of Parliamentary usage (or procedure) only. No record has been found of consent being withheld or inadvertently omitted by the Duchy of Cornwall. If such circumstances were to arise there is no authority to suggest that a Bill passed without consent would not pass into law. Consent only relates to the aspects of any Bill that affect the interest of the Duchy.[208] If consent were to be refused the question on the relevant stage of the Bill would not be proposed. The Duchy states its consent has never been withheld. It is not known if Bills have been changed to accommodate the views of the Duchy or the Duke of Cornwall. Of course, unlike the Queen, the relationship of the Duke of Cornwall with Ministers is not circumscribed by convention.

The consent of the Queen and the Prince of Wales is signified in Parliament by a Privy Counsellor usually at the Second Reading of a Bill.

The precise wording is:

"I have it in command from Her Majesty the Queen and His Royal Highness the Prince of Wales to acquaint the House that they, having been informed of the purport of the XXXXXX Bill, have consented to place their prerogative, so far as they are affected by the Bill, at the disposal of Parliament for the purposes of the Bill."[209]

Clearly for the consent of the Prince of Wales, in right of the Duchy of Cornwall, to be obtained he must first be told the purpose of the Bill and how it would affect the Duchy of

---

208 HC Reply by Sir George Young, Leader of the House 14th November 2011 col 498W

209 See for one of many examples, HL14th March 2006 column 1206

Cornwall. This is done by sending two copies of the Draft Bill to the Private Secretary to the Prince of Wales.

The earliest mention of Prince Charles giving consent was on 14 April 1970 in relation to "The Bolton Corporation Bill" and "The Plymouth and South West Devon Water Bill".[210]

Amongst the more surprising Bills which have required the consent of the Duchy have been the "Repayment of Advances of Remuneration Paid to Deceased Employees Bill",[211] the "Foreign Limitations Periods Bill"[212] and the "Taxation Provisions Relating to Nuclear Transfer Schemes Bill".[213]

The Prince of Wales, in right of the Duchy of Cornwall, has been consulted, as advised by the Government Departments concerned and after an online search of Hansard, on the following Bills for the period 2005–2012:

Session 2004–2005
- Companies (Audit, Investigations and Communities Enterprise) Bill
- Finance Bill
- Gambling Bill
- Hunting Bill
- Road Safety Bill

Session 2005–2006
- Charities Bill
- Commons Bill
- Company Law Reform Bill
- Natural Environment and Rural Communities Bill
- London Olympics Bill

---

210 See e mail from Parliamentary Archives to writer 21 April 2011
211 HC 10th May 1976 vol. 911 cc 189-191
212 HL 24th January 1984 vol. 447 cc 143
213 HC 13th July 2004 vol. 423 cc 1365-1379

Session 2007–2008

- Housing and Regeneration Bill
- Energy Bill
- Planning Bill
- Retail Development Bill

Session 2008–2009

- Apprenticeship Skills Children and Learning Bill
- Children's Rights Bill
- Coroners and Justice
- Co-operative and Community Benefit Societies and Credit Unions Bill
- Local Democracy, Economic Development and Construction Bill
- Marine and Coastal Access Bill
- Marine Navigation Aids Bill

Session 2010–2012

- Crown Benefices (Parish Representatives) Measure Bill
- Energy Bill
- Localism Bill
- Sovereign Grant Bill
- Wreck Removal Convention[214]

Establishing the above list of those Bills which have required the consent of the Duke of Cornwall has been much more difficult than was expected. There is no confidence the list is definitive.

---

214 Letter from Office of Parliamentary Counsel to writer 12 August 2010, e mail from House of Commons Archives 4th May 2011 and e mail from House of Commons 18th April 2012 to Christopher Hastings.

The right to be consulted

It is difficult to identify what aspect of the "hereditary revenues, personal property or other interests" of the Duchy is affected by some of the Bills about which the Prince of Wales was consulted. It is not apparent why the Prince was consulted on the Children's Rights Bill to take but one example. Examples of the circumstances which would give rise to the need for consent is given in Erskine May's Parliamentary Practice and are as follows:[215]

- Restrictions on the use that might be made of premises used by the Duchy;
- Creation of further statutory nuisances arising from land which have exposed the Duchy to legal proceedings;
- Changes to rules on *bona vacantia* and intestacy;
- Repeal of a protective provision which may have an adverse effect; and
- Application of legislation about construction contracts to contracts entered into on behalf of the Duke of Cornwall.

The criteria for consultation

Consultation with the Duchy of Cornwall and the consent of the Duke is not required for all proposed legislation. The next question is what factors are used to decide if the Duchy needs to be consulted?

A letter to the Cabinet Office resulted in the following:

"The Office does also have internal guidance that falls within the terms of your request. This information is however being withheld as falling with section 42 of that Act (legal professional privilege)...

The importance of this public interest was reaffirmed by the House of Lords in *Three Rivers DC v Bank of England* (No. 6) (2004) UKHL 48."[216]

---

215 Jack, Sir Malcolm, (Ed.) op. cit. pp 663—664
216 Letter Office of Parliamentary Counsel dated 19th September 2011

A request for an internal review was made and a reply was received on 16 November 2011[217] which, in summary, said the initial refusal had been considered and the original decision stood. The Duke and Duchy are, by Parliamentary usage entitled to be consulted when a Bill affects the "hereditary revenues, personal property or other interests" of the Duke of Cornwall. The Cabinet Office initially maintained we were not permitted to know how those terms are applied in practice such that the requirement for consent is triggered. In particular since it is only as Duke of Cornwall the heir to the throne claims particular constitutional privileges in other regards, at least theoretically, he a private citizen like all others, it is difficult to understand what "personal property or other interests" possessed by the Prince of Wales would require his consent.

After a complaint to the Information Commissioner the Cabinet Office produced a pamphlet entitled "Queen's or Prince's Consent" which can be downloaded from the Cabinet Office website.

Conclusion

The obtaining of the consent of the Prince of Wales, as Duke of Cornwall, described as "merely a usage of Parliament"[218] and "not a legal requirement", began more than one hundred and sixty years ago and possibly before that. The first record we have dates from 1848.[219] It is not unreasonable to suggest the process might actually have begun at that time since it corresponds with Prince Albert being in charge of the Duchy. It is the sort of change for which he would have canvassed. It serves as means to ensure that Duchy interests, particularly

---

217 Letter to writer from Head of Knowledge and Information Cabinet Office dated 16th November 2011

218 TNA LO 3/467—Duchy of Cornwall Land Tax and Valuation (1913)

219 Lords Journal lxxx p 736, HL/PO/JO/10/8/1692 and related to The West of England and South Wales Drainage Company Incorporation Bill

financial interests could be safeguarded. However, it would appear that the consultation and consent are now a requirement. If that is the case it is not clear how that obligation arose, what would happen if it were violated and who and by what means it would be enforced.

This "private estate" is consulted on proposed legislation. The criteria explaining what those terms mean in practice is withheld. It is not obvious when the Duchy will be consulted. Furthermore the public will not in the future be permitted to see any papers which explain how the process works.[220]

It is possible to argue Prince Charles is doing no more than is the right of any concerned citizen when he comments on legislation. Leaving aside the fact his opinions are likely to carry more weight than other citizens it is as Duke of Cornwall he has rights greater than those available to the rest of us. However, in exercising those rights he is not accountable.

---

220 Constitutional Reform and Governance Act 2010 schedule 7 means that correspondence between the heir to the throne and the second in line to the throne are not available under the Freedom of Information Act 2000. There is no longer a public interest test.

Chapter 8

The Duchy of Cornwall and Crown Immunity

The basis of Crown Immunity is the maxim: "The King/ Queen can do no wrong". There are three possible under- standings of the adage as follows. Whatever the King/Queen does cannot be wrong: The principle of "absolute perfection" which provides that, in law, the Sovereign is regarded as being incapable of thinking wrong or meaning to do an improper act. Next the Sovereign has no legal power to do wrong. Finally, as Maitland explained: "against the King, the law has no coercive power".[221] However the topic of Crown Immunity is complex. In 1235 Bracton in his Laws and Customs of England wrote *"Quod Rex non debet esse sub homine' sed sub Ded et Lege"*.[222]/[223] As early as 1561 in *Willion v Berkley* (1561)[224] it was settled in England that the Crown was bound by any statute that applied to it. It was also said in the same case: "When The King gives His consent He does not mean to prejudice Himself" An early formulation of the principle in English Law dates from 1604:

> *"Roy n'est lie per ascun statute, si il ne soit expressment nosme."*[225]

---

221 Tomkins, A., "Crown Privileges" in Sunkin, M., and Payne, S., *The Nature of the Crown* (1999) p. 176

222 That the King should not be under man, but under God and the law.

223 Bracton, *Laws and Customs of England* (1235)

224 *William v Berkley* (1561) (1 Plow. 223) (75 E.R. 339(KB))

Chitty describes it as:

> "the King is not bound by any Acts of Parliament as do not particularly and expressly mention him.
>
>   The King is impliedly bound by statutes passed for public good; the relief of the poor; the general advancement of learning, religion and justice; or to prevent fraud, injury or wrong."[226]

Diplock L.J. stated that:

> "the modern rule of construction of statutes is that the Crown... is not bound by a statute which imposes obligation or restraints on persons or in respect of property unless the statute says so expressly or by necessary implication."[227]

In Halsbury's Laws it is expressed as follows:

> "The Crown is not bound by statute unless the contrary is expressly stated, or unless there is a necessary implication to be drawn from the provisions of the Act that the Crown was intended to be bound, or there can somehow be gathered from the terms of the relevant Act an intention to that effect..."[228]

For an analysis conducted by the Office of Parliamentary Counsel see the pamphlet "Crown Application" available on the Cabinet Office Website.

---

225   *The King's Case* (1604) (7 Co Rep 32a) "the King is not bound by any statute unless he is expressly named in it"

226   Chitty, J., *A Treatise on the Law of the Prerogatives of the Crown* (1820) p 382

227   *BBC v Johns* (1965) Ch. At 78-79

228   Halsbury's Laws of England Volume 8(2) Constitutional Law and Human Rights para.384

It is striking that the document makes no mention of either the Duchy of Cornwall or Duke of Cornwall.

While there are those who may debate the basis of the principle of Crown Immunity and its extent, there is no doubt that it exists. It is questionable whether it can still be justified. It made sense when we had a "monarchical government" but that is no longer the case. A similar immunity is said to extend to the Duchy of Cornwall and it is this which will now be explored. This is not a theoretical question. Because of Crown Immunity the Duchy does not pay Capital Gains Tax, and, in respect of Duchy income, Prince Charles is not liable to income tax although he does make a voluntary payment equivalent to the amount that would be otherwise payable. As a further example there is a group on the Isles of Scilly called the Garrison Leasehold Group which is campaigning because the Leasehold Reform Act 1967, the Leasehold Reform, Housing and Urban Development Act 1993 and the Commonhold and Leasehold Reform Act 2002[229] do not apply to tenancies of the Duchy of Cornwall. Despite the fact they were not bound by the legislation, the Duchy agreed to enfranchisement of leases with certain exemptions one of which applied to the Isles of Scilly. The Duchy's concern is that properties would be owned by "off islanders" and become second homes, to the detriment of the islands.[230] The concern may be legitimate but the fact still remains that a right available to all other lessees is not available to Duchy tenants because of the application of Crown Immunity.[231]

It is difficult to establish when Crown Immunity began to be applied to the Duchy. There is no mention of it in the sixteenth

229 HC 3 April 2001 col. 176W
230 Letter Farrer & Co, solicitor to Duchy of Cornwall, dated 5 April 2001
231 Another example is the fact the Duchy of Cornwall is exempt from the various schemes relating to private sewers and private lateral drains which arise under the Water Industry Act 1991 and the Water Act 2003

century book by Sir William Staunford's "The Pleas of the Crown"[232] or Sir Matthew Hale's "The Prerogatives of the Crown"[233] published in the seventeenth century or specifically in Chitty's "Treatise on the Law of the Prerogatives of the Crown"[234] issued in 1822. Although the latter did say:

"So a grant from the King to the Prince (of Wales) does not make alienation from the Crown, for the land continues parcel of the Crown."[235]

Lord Redesdale observed in 1817 that:

"it will be difficult to find that the Prince of Wales as Duke of Cornwall stands in any other relation than that of a Subject considering him merely as Duke of Cornwall."[236]

The Land Taxes Act 1798 applied to the Duchy of Cornwall. Indeed the Duchy was specifically permitted to dispose of property in order to be able to pay the tax.[237] The Duchy in the nineteenth century sought to re-establish its right to wreck which brought it into dispute with the Board of Trade and holders of various manorial rights. In particular the Duchy claimed the Merchant Shipping Act 1854 did apply to Cornwall and the Board of Trade's investigation into wrecks within the County was illegal. The matter was referred to the

---

232 Staunford, Sir William *The Pleas of the Crown* (1560)

233 Hale, Sir Matthew, *The Prerogatives of the King* (1976 Written 1640-1676)

234 Chitty, op. cit.

235 Chitty, op. cit. p 405 He shows as authority for the proposition *Comyns Digest Roy G* which in turn cites *Palmer Reports*.

236 TNA TS 27/818—Treasure Trove; Duchy claim mining rights (1907—1932)

237 Haslam, G., "Modernisation" in Gill, C., *The Duchy of Cornwall* (1987) p. 48

Law Officers who determined the Act did apply to the Duchy thus they did not enjoy the right to Crown Immunity.[238]

In an issue which arose in 1855, when the Duchy was managed by the Crown, with regard to the payment of the Queen's Remembrancer fees[239] it was concluded that the Prince of Wales was a subject suing for his own benefit and not suing "on the part of the Crown or the Public" and was in the same position as any other suitor "not the Crown or a Public Department of Revenue". Therefore the provisions of the Exchequer Court Act 1842 did apply and the Duchy did not enjoy Crown Immunity. In that case the Attorney and Solicitor General stated:

> "It therefore appears to us *incorrect to say that the interest of the Crown in these Revenues is permanent subject to the contingent claim of a HRH whenever a Prince of Wales exists… it is the interest of the Crown which is contingent…*" (emphasis added)

The Law Officers are saying it is the Duke of Cornwall to whom the Duchy reverts with the Crown having a contingent interest rather than the reverse.

Notes on the Civil List were prepared for the Treasury in 1897 they record "exemption from taxation is part of the Royal prerogative."[240] They go on to say:

> "The taxation paid in respect of the Duchies of Lancaster and Cornwall is shown in the annual accounts of these Duchies, and consists of property tax (for which

---

238 TNA BT 243/262—The Duchy of Cornwall: Legislation relating to right of wrecks of the sea (1856-1985). For full discussion see Pearce, C., *Cornish Wrecking 1700- 1860* The Boydell Press (2010) p 182

239 TNA TS 25/829—Whether fees payable to Queen's Remembrancer (1865)

240 TNA T 38/837—Civil List Notes "The Welby Papers" (1897)

certain sums are allowed annually to the tenants of the Duchies) land tax and 'other taxes'."

There is no reference, which might be expected, in what is a comprehensive review, to Crown Immunity applying to the Duchy of Cornwall.

In 1899 Sir Edward Walter Hamilton of the Treasury wrote a letter concerning property rating of members of the Royal family in which he said:

> "it is a well known maxim that the Crown is not bound by any Act of Parliament except by express enactment; *there is no such maxim applicable to the Heir Apparent, or any other member of the Royal Family. I doubt, therefore whether the Executive Government could exempt expressly the Prince from any part of the Income Tax now paid by him without the authority of Parliament.*"[241] (emphasis added)

The only detailed analysis of this topic, as far as can be established, was conducted by the Solicitor for the Board of the Inland Revenue in 1913. (See Appendix VII) The specific question was whether a provision of the Finance Act 1910 applied to the Duchy. The general point was whether:

> "the Prince of Wales possesses the same prerogatives as the King (who) is not bound by statute unless expressly named, the Prince of Wales either absolutely or at all events so far as the lands of the Duchy of Cornwall are concerned, is not bound…"[242]

---

241 TNA T 168/71—Papers relating to taxation and property rating of members of the Royal Family (1899-1904)

242 TNA LO 3/467—Duchy of Cornwall Land Tax and Valuation (1913)

In summary the line of reasoning advanced by the Board was: Crown Immunity was a prerogative right different in substance from other rights, for example royal fish, wreck and so on, granted to the Duchy. The King under the Bill of Rights 1688 had no power by prerogative to suspend laws as they applied to the Prince of Wales and if such a grant existed it would be "inoperative". The Inland Revenue could find no authority "directly laying down the proposition that the Duke of Cornwall... is not bound by statute unless expressly named... "

The Duchy argued that:

1 The prerogative rights of the Duchy are identical with those of the Crown;
2 Express mention is made of the Duchy in Acts of Parliament when those Acts are intended to apply to the Duchy;
3 Duchy lands are treated in the same way as Crown lands; and
4 The fact that Duchy lands are Crown lands mean the same principles apply.

The Board conceded that the procedure of signifying consent in Parliament had been applied to Duchy lands in the same way as Crown lands but that was a matter of Parliamentary usage—a view shared latterly by the Information Commissioner. There were no instructions to that effect and the position "might, and probably would, vary according to circumstances." They also acknowledged that it had been the practice to deal with Duchy lands expressly in Acts of Parliament but argued it would be going too far to say that without an express statutory reference, Acts would not bind the Duchy. In this regard they quoted *The Attorney General to the*

Prince of Wales v Mayor of Plymouth (1754)[243] and *The Attorney General to the Prince of Wales v St Aubyn* (1811).[244]

The Inland Revenue acknowledged that the strongest argument put forward by the Duchy was that Duchy lands were Crown lands and therefore the same prerogatives applied to both. In *St Aubyn* it was said:

> "Duchy lands are part of them (Crown Lands) as a member of the Royal establishment."

Rowe v Brenton (1828)[245] was quoted at length as follows:

> "I am clearly of the opinion that the Duke of Cornwall is not to be considered as a private subject; when there is no Duke of Cornwall, the Duchy belongs to the Crown… when there is a Duke in all these matters the interest of the Crown is equally concerned."
>
> "considering the very peculiar nature of the Duchy of Cornwall, whether the Duchy be vested in the Crown or in the Duke, the Crown has a peculiar interest in it at all times…"

It was, therefore, conceded on behalf of the Inland Revenue that the Crown retains some special and peculiar interest and Duchy lands in the hands of the Prince are not precisely in the same position as lands in the hands of a subject. However, to admit a special interest of the Crown is different from acknowledging that the special prerogative of the Crown applied.

---

243 Attorney General to the Prince of Wales v Mayor of Plymouth (1754) (Wight 134)

244 Attorney General to the Prince of Wales v St Aubyn (1811) (Wight 167)

245 *Rowe v Brenton* (1828) (8 B & C 737) p 1224

The problem caused by the situation which arises when there is no Duke and is managed by the Crown was explored. It was suggested by the Inland Revenue that during those times when there was no Duke or no Duke of full age Crown Immunity did apply to the Duchy.

The Law Officers gave their opinion that:

> "We are of the opinion that the same principles which render the provisions of an Act of Parliament inapplicable to the Crown unless the Crown is expressly named apply also to the Prince of Wales in his capacity as Duke of Cornwall. This result arises from the peculiar title of the Prince of Wales to the Duchy of Cornwall."

The Law Officers did not then go on to explain what, in their view, was the nature of this "peculiar title". As Mr Wilson said during the Select Committee Hearing in 1971–72:

> "the judgement was very short and a little inscrutable because it referred to the peculiar or special nature of the Duchy of Cornwall, and did not go on to say what was peculiar or special…"[246]

By way of contrast in 1904 King Edward VII objected to paying income tax. Papers in the National Archives record:

> "it is probable that the arrangement about income tax rankles… this was the feeling of Queen Victoria.… She felt that She had been rather "let in" with regard to it.… She had been prevailed upon by Sir Robert Peel to subject Herself to tax by way of example to Her

---

246   House of Commons *Report from Select Committee on the Civil List* 1971-72, HC29
      p 669

people… instead of submitting Herself to a temporary tax, She had unknowingly agreed to pay tax which lasted throughout the remaining 59 years of her reign.… This She resented and the present King only agreed to continue under protest."[247]

The Duchy of Cornwall like the Sovereign had paid income tax from 1842. In 1910 the Sovereign ceased to pay. If the same privileges extended to the Duke of Cornwall why did he continue paying the tax?

Conclusion

While the Solicitor to the Board of the Inland Revenue acknowledged there are complicating issues his proposition is as follows. The prerogative of Crown Immunity is a special right differing from other prerogative rights which can and have been granted by the Crown. The granting of such a prerogative would require specific words. There are no documents by which the Crown granted such a prerogative. Furthermore even if such a document existed it would be ineffective because of the Bill of Rights 1688 which prevents the Crown by prerogative suspending the application of laws to the Prince of Wales. Because the Duchy oscillates between the Crown and Duchy the Law Officers concluded the Duchy did enjoy this special prerogative. It must be assumed the "peculiar title" to which the Law Officers referred arises from the fact the Duchy "reverts" to the Crown when there is no Duke. Certainly the Great Charter of 17 March 1337 says if there is no Duke:

"the same Duchy with the Castles Boroughs Towns and all other things abovesaid *shall* revert to us to be

247 TNA T168/71 Papers relating to taxation and property rating of members of the Royal Family (1899-1904)

retained in the hands of the Kingdom of England until there appear such Son…" (emphasis added)

Mr Iain Wright, M.P., Under Secretary of State in the Department of Communities, and Local Government explained it as follows:

> "even though it is managed as a private estate, the Duchy of Cornwall can only be held by the eldest son of the reigning monarch, and if there is no son, then it *reverts* to the Crown. I believe this is self-explanatory where the link to the Crown is concerned."[248] (emphasis added)

Erskine May in its explanation of the need to obtain consent in respect of Bills before Parliament explains the need for consent because of the "reversion" of the Duchy when there is no Duke.

The principle would appear to be that anything which affects the Duchy, particularly to its detriment, for example, the imposition of tax, has a consequence for the Sovereign because the Crown enjoys the right of reversion.

There are difficulties with the basis of the Law Officers opinion, in so far is it can be discerned, and others who share their logic. The Solicitor to the Board of the Inland Revenue and the Law Officers would appear to have been unaware of the comments in the House of Lords and the disputes which arose in the nineteenth century. The question of Mines Royal, a disagreement which started in the nineteenth century and is still unresolved, has been mentioned already. The Duchy claimed Mines Royal; the Crown Estate has resisted the claim because it is a prerogative right which is so "high a character"

---

248   Letter Iain Wright M.P. Under Secretary of State Dept. of Communities and Local Government to Andrew George M.P. 16th June 2009

and could only be passed, the Law Officers argued, by express words. It is not in doubt that the Crown could grant such a right but it has not done so and it could not pass by implication. The Law Officers agreed with the Crown in an opinion which the Duchy did not and does not accept. Unquestionably the right to Mines Royal, while a significant prerogative right, is a lesser right to that of Crown Immunity yet in the case of Mines Royal it did not pass while Crown Immunity does.

Next there is the question of the "reversion" to the Crown. It is important to emphasize that the Duchy does not "escheat" to the Crown. It is never absorbed in the Crown. Sir George Harrison in 1837 wrote that the King was "duty bound to maintain the Duchies and transmit them to his successors". He suggested the Sovereign, when there was no Duke or the Duke was a minor was invested with the character of a trustee and "The Sovereign trustee could in fact if not in theory do wrong if he bargained away the Duchy of Cornwall."[249] The Duchy itself refers to the "trust" provisions of the founding Charters.[250] The Attorney General to H.R.H. the Prince of Wales likened the Duchy to a trust created under the Settled Land Act 1925.[251]

If we pursue the analogy of the Duchy being like a trust, the trustee then is either the Sovereign or the Duke of Cornwall. The beneficial interests are the life tenant, the Duke of Cornwall, with the Sovereign having a contingent interest. When the Sovereign is trustee then, as Harrison implied, he or she holds the Duchy as legal owner but not as absolute owner. That is to say he or she holds the property in accordance with the founding documents for the benefit of the beneficiaries

---

249 Harrison, Sir George, *Memoir respecting the Hereditary Revenues of the Crown and the Revenues of the Duchies of Cornwall and Lancaster* (1837) p 36

250 Duchy of Cornwall Annual Accounts 31st March 2012

251 *Michael Bruton v Information Commissioner, The Duchy of Cornwall and The Attorney General to HRH the Prince of Wales* (2011) (EA/2010/0182) p 17.

from time to time. Whether it is the Sovereign or the Duke who is entitled to the income from the Duchy, they at all times have an "interest" in the estate and not in the estate itself which is a separate entity. To import the rights and privileges which a person enjoys personally, even the Sovereign, or by virtue of his or her position to his or her role as trustee is a dubious proposition. This logic would suggest that as the Sovereign has the right to Mines Royal, when the Sovereign is trustee then the Duchy would also enjoy Mines Royal which the Law Officers say it does not.

As a further demonstration of the restricted nature of the Monarch's interest in the land held by the Duchy it continues to be held in fee. In *The Attorney General v The Mayor and Commonalty of the Borough of Plymouth* (1754) Chief Baron Parker said

> "It is clear, that the Crown does *not take an absolute fee, but only a qualified fee* till the birth of the King's eldest son he takes a fee; but it is only a qualified fee till he comes to the Crown, or till his own death…"[252] (emphasis added)

When there is no Duke of Cornwall the Crown holds the lands of the Duchy of Cornwall in qualified fee from itself.

In 1833 when the Duchy had reverted to the Crown a dispute arose regarding the Isles of Scilly in which it was concluded the title rested with the Duchy. In 1854, when the Duke of Cornwall was a minor and the Duchy was managed by the Crown a disagreement arose regarding the Queens Remembrancer's fees. If the Duchy had become absorbed in the Crown when there was no Duke or the Duke was a minor then these disputes could not have arisen. The Sovereign

---

[252] *Attorney General to HRH the Prince of Wales, Duke of Cornwall v The Mayor and Commonalty of Plymouth and others* (1754) (Wight 134) p 1214

THE DUCHY OF CORNWALL AND CROWN IMMUNITY

would have either disputed with himself or Crown Immunity would have applied.

Another example is the matter of *Bona Vacantia*. Even when there is no Duke or the Duke is a minor the right to *Bona Vacantia* continues to be dealt with separately by the Treasury Solicitor on behalf of the Crown and the solicitors to the Duchy of Cornwall on behalf of the Duchy. The Crown and the Duchy were and are distinct. A telling observation was made by the Clerk to the Crown in 1889 during the discussions about the production of a Royal Warrant for the Lord Warden of the Stannaries to be able to summon a militia was that the warrant could not suggest the Crown confirmed the appointment of the Lord Warden that would be a "proceeding which would be "*ultra viries*" (beyond the powers of) and "an encroachment on the jurisdiction of the Duke of Cornwall".[253]

Halsbury's Laws of England summarizes the situation. It says:

> "Because the monarch is a separate person from... the Duke of Cornwall there can be a valid lease or conveyance between them.... When the Duchy of Cornwall is vested in the Crown rights formerly enjoyed over one estate for the benefit of the other will not merge."[254]/[255]

There is only one reported case which directly addresses the question of Crown Immunity and the Duchy of Cornwall, *Hobbs v Weeks* (1950).[256] This was a County Court case

---

253 TNA C 197/18—Commission for the management of the Duchy of Cornwall (1827 -1889)

254 *R v Inhabitants of Hermitage* (1692) (Carth. 239) (90 ER 743)

255 Halsbury's Laws of England Volume 12(1) section 213 Relations between aspects of the Crown.

256 *Hobbs v Weeks* (1950) (100 L.J. 178) p 178

therefore not a precedent, in which Judge Wethered at Wells County Court held:

"That when the lands of the Duchy of Cornwall are vested in the Crown (as they have been since the accession of Edward VIII) the Rent Restriction Acts do not apply to premises comprised in them."

This decision would suggest that when not in the Crown the Rent Restriction Acts would then have applied.

There is no specific grant by the Sovereign of Crown Immunity to the Duchy of Cornwall anymore than there is an Act of Parliament extending Crown Immunity to the Duchy. The right is not mentioned by Staunford, Hale and there is a qualified reference, only, in Chitty all of whom are regarded as authorities in these matters. The evidence suggests that in the nineteenth century, as demonstrated by the Merchant Shipping Act 1854 and the Exchequer Court Act 1842, it was not assumed the Duchy enjoyed Crown Immunity. The opinion of the Law Officers in 1913 is inconsistent with the opinions offered with regard to Mines Royal and others and is based on a fundamental misunderstanding of the relationship of the Duchy to the Crown.

By virtue of the Duchy's right to Crown Immunity a "private estate" enjoys substantial privileges without there being any clear basis upon which those privileges are founded. There is an opinion which is not consistent with the previous opinions offered by the same Department or past practice and which does not address the very detailed issues raised by the person who sought the opinion.

Chapter 9

Devon Laws

"The custom of bounding in Devon... has not been abrogated"[257]

Introduction
Until this point we have been primarily concerned with the Laws of Cornwall. However Devon retains some rights and the Duchy of Cornwall maintains some privileges in Devon which are noteworthy.

The Devon Stannaries
We have seen the laws relating to the Stannaries of Cornwall extended to the whole of Cornwall. That is not true of Devon. There were four Stannary Towns—Chagford, Tavistock, Ashburton and Plympton—whose precise boundaries were never defined as far as this writer is aware.

The Great Court of the Devon Tinners
The earliest records for the Great Court date from 1520. This compares with 1588 for the equivalent body in Cornwall. It met in 1520, 1532, 1533, 1552, 1574, 1600, 1688, and 1703.[258] According to one writer the Great Court met for the last time in 1786.[259]

---

257 Halsbury's Laws of England/Mines Minerals and Quarries Vol. 31/Local Rights and Customs/Tin Bounding in Cornwall and Devon para. 592

258 Pennington, R., "Stannary Law" (1988) *Bulletin of the Peak District Mines Historical Society* vol. 10, No 4

259 Greeves, T., "The Great Courts or Parliaments of the Devon Tinners" (1987) The Devon Association Vol. 119 p 143-166

The Great Court of the Tinners of Devon consisted of ninety six jurates, twenty four being chosen from each of the Devon Stannaries. The jurates were chosen by the tinners which term included miners, tin work owners and other concerned with the tin mining industry. The Great Court did not enjoy the right of veto which had been granted to Cornwall's Convocation.

If, as explored in an earlier chapter, the Convocation of the Tinners of Cornwall is, in theory, capable of being summoned the same arguments must apply to Great Court.

Bounding

The custom of tin bounding in Devon was generally similar to that in Cornwall. It fell into disuse in the eighteenth century but has not been abrogated. Under the Devon custom a tinner could work tin existing in any land in the county other than meadows, orchards, gardens, houses or grain or corn land or certain woods or groves. The woods or groves referred to were those where the working would necessitate the overthrowing of 20 timber trees of 20 years growth.[260] He could work in the excepted land with the consent of the owner and occupier. If such consent were given the owner and occupier were entitled to a share of the produce. Tin bounds were to be renewed yearly.[261]

Right to Sea-Sand

People dwelling in Devon have the same right, if they still exist, of taking sea-sand for agricultural purposes as those who dwell in Cornwall.

---

260 Pearce, T., *The Laws and Customs of the Stannaries* (1725) p 248
261 Halsbury's Laws of England Mines, Minerals and Quarries Vol. 31 para. 592

Devon Waters

The Duchy of Cornwall owns the "fundus" or navigable river bed and foreshore of the Tamar, the Salcombe and Kingsbridge estuaries, the River Dart and River Avon. Clearly these are highly remunerative.

Chapter 10

Conclusion

For anyone interested in law the United Kingdom offers opportunities for study which few other places can rival. It is the survival of local rules and customs which are, in my view, particularly fascinating. Nowhere is this evidenced more than in Cornwall and to a lesser extent Devon and the Isles of Scilly. Cornwall's constitutional relationship with England is a matter of heated debate[262] and this Introductory text has not sought to address those questions. What is indisputable is that the Duchy of Cornwall has an association with Cornwall which is truly extraordinary. As I have tried to explain it is not an exaggeration to say that the Duchy is Cornwall in the sense that it owns the land of Cornwall "allodially" or has in "fee" from the Crown.

A number of rights enjoyed by the Duchy of Cornwall in relation to Cornwall at first glance seem rather quaint but the economic benefits which accrue to the Duchy which, based on my personal knowledge they assert with some determination, should not be underestimated. For example, the right to a significant part of the foreshore and the fundus of the rivers in Cornwall and indeed Devon generates considerable income. Just consider, for a moment, the surf schools and others who pay rent to the Duchy and the yacht owners who pay mooring fees on the Helston. Then there are the percentage of the tolls which the Duchy receives from those using the Torpoint Ferry and King Harry's Ferry. Similarly the right of *Escheat* and *Bona*

---

262 See Angarrack, J., *Breaking the Chains* (1999), *Our Future is History* (2002), *Scat t'Larrups* (2008)

Vacantia offer substantial financial benefits as does the Duchy's relationship with the Isles of Scilly.

The benefit to the Duchy in enjoying the requirement that, in certain circumstances, Parliament must seek its approval for proposed Bills is a means, should they wish to exercise it, of protecting its economic interests. Similarly its, in my view, contentious claim to "Crown Immunity" directly impacts on groups of people living in Cornwall and the Isles of Scilly.

The Duchy, in my opinion, retains the right, one may even say duty, to summon the Convocation of the Tinners of Cornwall and by extension the Great Court of the Tinners of Devon. As we have seen Professor Pennington 39 years gave his opinion that, in certain circumstances, the Duke of Cornwall could be obliged to recall the Convocation. Be that as it may it is a right which is not likely to be exercised voluntarily but if it were to happen I, for one, would be pleased to assist in its reassembly.

There is no doubt the right to "bound" within Cornwall and, I will admit, to my surprise in Devon still exists. It is an entitlement which to my certain knowledge is still exercised certainly in Cornwall and can be the cause of some inconvenience to the authorities. It is also possible to demonstrate that one is a "privileged tinner" and, therefore, claim the benefit of the 1305 Tinners Charter.

I have considered the question of sea-sand and whether it is still permissible to remove it from the beaches of Devon and Cornwall for agricultural purposes. People do remove sea-sand in Cornwall although not in Devon as far as I know. Does the right still exist in law? Frankly I am not sure. There is certainly an argument under the Commons Registration Act 1965 it does not but, as far as I know, that issue has never been placed before the Courts in which cases have been heard so the question must be regarded as unresolved.

My hope in writing this book has been to interest and intrigue such that others will take up and extend my researches. In addition I look forward to those who knowledge is greater than mine contacting me so this work may be refined, improved and extended resulting in as consequence a "textbook" for the Laws relating to Cornwall.

John Kirkhope
2014

Appendix I

The Cornish Stannary Charters
and
Resolutions of the Privy Council

Charter of Liberties to the Tinners of Cornwall and
Devon (1201)

Charter of Liberties to the Tinners of Cornwall
(1305)

Charter of Confirmation to the Tinners of
Cornwall (1402)

Grant or Patent of Pardon and Immunities to the
Tinners, Bounders, and Possessors of Works of
Tin of Cornwall (1508)

Resolutions of the Judges in 1608

Resolutions of the Privy Council 1632

CHARTER OF LIBERTIES
to the
TINNERS OF CORNWALL AND DEVON

3 JOHN[263]
(1201)

The King to the Archbishops, etc., greeting.... John, by the grace of God, King of England, etc., to the archbishops, bishops, abbots, earls, barons, judges, sheriffs, foresters, and to all our bailiffs and faithful people, greeting. Be it known that we have conceded that all tin miners of Cornwall and Devon are quit of all local pleas of the natives as long as they work for the profit of our farm or for the marks for our new tax; for the Stannaries are on our demesne. And they may dig for tin, and for turf for smelting it, at all times freely and peaceably without hindrance from any man, on the moors and in the fiefs of bishops, abbots, and earls, as they have been accustomed to do. And they may buy faggots to smelt the tin, without waste of forest, and they may divert streams for their work just as they have been accustomed to do by ancient usage. Nor shall they desist from their work by reason of any summons, except those of the chief warden of the Stannaries or his bailiffs. We have granted also that the chief warden of the Stannaries and his bailiffs have plenary power over the miners to do justice to them and to hold them to the law. And if it should happen that any of the miners ought to be seized and imprisoned for breach

---

263 Lewis, G. R *The Stannaries—A Study of the Medieval Tin Miners of Cornwall and Devon* (1908) p 238

of the law they should be received in our prisons; and if any of them should become a fugitive or outlaw let his chattels be delivered to us by the hands of the warden of the Stannaries because the miners are of our farm and always in our power.

Moreover, we concede to our treasurer and the weighers, so that they might be more faithful and attentive to our service in guarding our treasure in market towns, that they shall be quit in all towns in which they stay of aids and tallages as long as they are in our service as treasurers and weighers; for they have and can have nothing else throughout the year for their services to us. Witnesses, etc.

CHARTER of LIBERTIES
to the
TINNERS OF CORNWALL

33 Edward I[264]
(1305)

"For the tinners in Cornwall.—The King to the Archbishops, greeting. Know ye, that for the improvement of our Stannaries in the County of Cornwall and/or the tranquillity and advantage of our tinners of the same, we have granted for us and for our heirs, that all the tinners aforesaid working those Stannaries, which are our demesnes, whilst they work in the same Stannaries, shall he free and quit of pleas of natives, and of all pleas and suits in any wise touching the Court of us, or of our heirs, so that they shall not answer before any justices or ministers of us, or our heirs, of any plea or suit within the aforesaid Stannaries arising, unless before the custos of our Stannaries aforesaid, who for the time being shall be, excepting pleas of land, and of life, and of members, nor shall they depart from their works for the summons of any of the ministers of us, or of our heirs, unless by summons of our said custos; and they shall be quiet of all tallages, toll stallages, aids, and other customs whatsoever, in the towns, ports, fairs, and markets within the county aforesaid, for their own goods. We have granted also the said tinners that they may dig tin, and turves to melt tin, anywhere in the lands, moors, and wastes of us, and of others whomsoever, in the county aforesaid, and divert water and water courses for the works of the Stannaries aforesaid, where and when it shall be necessary, and buy wood

264   Concanen, G *A Report of the Trial at Bar Rowe v Brenton* (1830) Appendix L

to melt the tin, as they have been accustomed, without
hindrance of us, or of our heirs, bishops, abbots, priors, earls,
barons, or others whomsoever, and that our custos aforesaid,
or his deputy, shall hold all pleas between the tinners aforesaid
arising, and also arising between them and other strangers, for
all trespassers, suits, and contracts, made in the places in which
they work within the Stannaries aforesaid, and that the same
custos shall have full power to judge the tinners aforesaid, and
other strangers, in such pleas, and to do justice to the parties,
as shall be right and heretofore used in the same Stannaries;
and if any of the tinners aforesaid shall have transgressed in
anything/or which they ought to he imprisoned, they shall be
arrested by the custos aforesaid, and in our prison of
Lostwythiel, and not elsewhere, shall he kept and detained
until, according to law and the custom of our kingdom, they
shall be delivered; and if any of the tinners aforesaid, upon any
fact within the county aforesaid, not touching the Stannaries
aforesaid, shall put himself upon an inquisition of the county,
one half of the jurors of such inquisition shall he of the tinners
aforesaid, and the other half of strangers. If concerning a fact
wholly touching the Stannaries aforesaid, the inquisitions shall
he made as they have heretofore been accustomed; and if any
of the same tinner shall be fugitive or outlaw or shall have
made any default for which he ought to lose his chattels, those
chattels shall be appraised by the custos aforesaid, and our
coroner of the county aforesaid, and by them at the next towns
shall be delivered to answer thereupon to us and our heirs,
before our justices itinerant in the county aforesaid. We will,
moreover and firmly command that all the tin, as well white
as black, wheresoever it shall he found and wrought in the
county aforesaid, shall be weighed at Lostwyhiel, Bodmynyan,
Liskeret, Trevern, or Helleston, by our weights for this ordered
and signed, upon forfeiture of all the tin aforesaid; and that the
whole of the same tin shall he coined in the same towns every

year before the custos aforesaid, before the day of St Michael, in September under forfeiture aforesaid. And we have granted for us, and for our heirs, that all our tinners afore said may lawfully sell all their tin so weighed to whomsoever they will in the town aforesaid, by making to us and to our heirs the coinage and other customs due and used, unless we, or our heirs, shall buy: wherefore we will and firmly command for us and for our heirs, that our tinners at aforesaid shall have all the liberties, free customs, and acquittances above written, and that they, without hindrance or impediment of us, or of our heirs, justices, escheators, sheriffs, or other bailiffs or ministers, whomsoever the same shall reasonably enjoy inform aforesaid.

These being witnesses, the venerable fathers, W, Bishop of Coventry and Lichfield; S Bishop of Salisbury, J Bishop of Karlisles, Henry de Lacy Earl of Lincoln; Ralph de Monte Hermerio, Earl of Gluceston and Hertford: Humphrey de Bohim, Earl of Hereford and Essex; Adomar de Valence: Hugh le Dispenser: John de Hastings, and others. Given by our hand, at Westminster the l0th day of April. in the 33rd year of our reign.

CHARTER OF CONFIRMATION
to the
TINNERS OF CORNWALL

3 Henry IV[265]
(1402)

The King, to all to whom, etc., greeting. We have inspected letters-patent of the Lord Richard, late King of England, the second after the conquest, our predecessor, late made in these words—Richard, by the grace of God, King of England and France, and Lord of Ireland, to all to whom these our present letters shall come greeting, we have inspected letters-patent of the Lord Edward, King of England and, our grandfather, in these words—Edward, by the grace of God, King of England and France, and Lord of Ireland, to all to whom these present letters shall come greeting, it appears to us by the inspection of the rolls of our Chancery that we lately caused our charter, under the seal which we then used in England, to be made in these words—Edward, by the grace of God, King of England and France, and Lord of Ireland, to the archbishops, bishops, abbots, priors, earls, barons, justices, sheriffs, reeves, ministers, and to all his bailiffs and faithful people, greeting, it appears to us by inspection of the rolls of Chancery of the Lord Edward, late King of England, our grandfather, that the same, our grandfather, made his charter in these words—*(reciting the charter 33 Edward 1)*—We also grant of the same, our grandfather aforesaid, and all and singular in the charter aforesaid contained, holding firm and valid the same for us and our heirs as much as in us is at the request of Edward I of Cornwall, and

---

265   Concanen, G., *A Report of the Trial at Bar Rowe v Brenton* (1830) Appendix L

STANNARY CHARTERS AND RESOLUTIONS OF THE PRIVY COUNCIL

Earl of Chester, our most dear son, to the stanners aforesaid, by the tenor of these presents, have granted, accepted, and confirmed as in the charter aforesaid, is reasonably accepted, and as the same stanners and their ancestors, and predecessors, the liberties aforesaid, from the time of the grant thereof by virtue of the charter aforesaid, have always heretofore been accustomed reasonably to use and enjoy. These being witnesses, the venerable father John, Archbishop of Canterbury, primate of all England; Simon, Bishop of Ely; Robert, Bishop of Chichester; John de Warren, Earl of Surrey and Sussex; Robert Parnying, our chancellor; William de Cusance, our treasurer; Ralph de Stafford, steward of our household; and others. Given by the hand of the aforesaid Duke Guardian of England, at Kenyngton, the nineteenth day of October, in the sixteenth year of our reign of England, and of France the third. We, moreover, the tenor of the charter aforesaid, under the seal which we now use in England, by the tenor of these presents, have caused to be exemplified in testimony whereof these our letters we have caused to be made patent. Witness myself at Westminster, the twenty-fourth day of January, in the eighteenth year of our reign of England, and of France the third. We moreover the grand wills and precepts aforesaid, and all and singular in the said letters contained, holding firm and valid the same for us and for our heirs, as much as in us is, do accept, approve, ratify, and to the aforenamed stanners, by the tenor of these presents, do grant and confirm, as the letters aforesaid reasonably witness, and as the same stanners and their predecessors, the liberties aforesaid, from the time of grant of the same, have always been accustomed to use and enjoy; in testimony whereof these our letters we have caused to be made patent. Witness myself at Westminster, the, first day of July, in the eighteenth year of our reign. We more over the grants, wills, and precepts aforesaid, and all and singular in the said letters contained, holding firm and valid the same for us and for our heirs, as much as in us is, to the aforenamed stanners, by the tenor of these presents do grant and confirm as the letters aforesaid reasonably witness, and as the same stanners and their predecessors, the liberties aforesaid reasonably witness, from the time of the grant of the same, have been accustomed reasonably to use and enjoy: in testimony whereof these our letters we have caused to be made patent. Witness myself at Westminster, the nineteenth day of May.

GRANT or PATENT OF PARDON AND IMMUNITIES
to the
TINNERS, BOUNDERS AND POSSESSORS OF WORKS OF TIN OF CORNWALL

Anno 23 Henry VII[266]
(1508)

The King to all to whom, &c., greeting. Know ye, that we of our special grace, and of our certain knowledge and mere motion, have pardoned, remised and released, and by these presents do pardon, remise, and release, to Robert Willoughby, Lord de Broke, John Mowne, of Hall, in the County of Cornwall, Esq., (and then follow about 1500 names,) and to every of them, otherwise called tinners, bounders, or possessors of works of tin, and to the bounder or possessor of any tinwork in the County of Cornwall, who have not or hath not introduced the names of new possessors, or a new possessor of any tinwork newly bounded, with the names of the works, in the next Court of Stannary after the bounding aforesaid, showing the names or name of the possessors or possessor of the same works or work, of tin, with the metes and bounds of the said works or work as well in length as in breadth, to the possessors or possessor of any houses or house, called blowing houses or a blowing house, in the County of Cornwall, who have not or hath not introduced the number of all and singular the pieces

---

266   Concanen, G *A Report of the Trial at Bar Rowe v Brenton* (1830) Appendix L

AN INTRODUCTION TO THE LAWS OF CORNWALL, SCILLY, AND DEVON

of tin in the Exchequer at Lostwithiel, yearly, at the time of every coinage, with the names or name of all and singular the possessors or possessor of the same houses or house, called blowing-houses or a blowing house, with the names or name of all and singular the blowers or workers, blower or worker of the same pieces or parcels of tin blown or wrought in the same houses or house, called blowing houses or blowing house, at the time of the coinage there, to the tinners or tinner, buyers or buyer of black or white tin, and to the makers or maker of white tin, who have not or hath not introduced the marks or mark of the possessors or possessor of the said tin, in the said Exchequer at Lostwithiel, to be impressed, put, or written in a certain book of signatures or marks, being in the said Exchequer, before the same possessors or possessor shall sign the said tin with the said mark to the tinners or buyers, tinner or buyer of black or white tin, to the changers or changer of the marks or mark of any possessors or possessor so impressed, put or written to the said book of marks, being in the said Exchequer, to the tinners or buyers, tinner or buyer of black tin, to the blowers or workers, blower or worker of false or hard tin, as well with the letter H; as without the letter H; and to the blowers or workers, blower or worker of white tin from their own black tin, and to every of them, by whatsoever other means or additions of names or occupations they or any of them are or may be known—all transgressions, contempts, impeachments, forfeitures, concealments, fines, pains, imprisonments, amerciaments, debts, and losses adjudged or to be adjudged, abuses, retentions, and offences, against the form of any statutes, ordinances, provisions, restrictions, or proclamations, by us or by our progenitors, &c., whatsoever authority before this time made, &c. (*This charter then proceeds to the following effect*)—that no statutes, acts, &c., hereafter issuing, to be made within the county aforesaid nor without, to the prejudice or exoneration of the same tinners, workers of black and white tin, &c., or of any persons or person whomsoever meddling with any black or white tin in the county aforesaid, their heirs, or successors, &c., unless there be first thereunto called twenty and four good and lawful men, from the four Stannaries within the County of Cornwall, to be elected, &c.

So that no statute, ordinance, provision or proclamation, hereafter to be made by us, our heirs or successors, or by the aforesaid Prince of Wales, Duke of Cornwall for the time being, or by our council, or the council of our said heirs or successors, or of the said Prince, be made, unless with the assent and consent of the aforesaid twenty and four men, so to be elected and named, &c., and the parties aforesaid, their heirs, &c., shall be hereafter otherwise charged, &c., towards us, our heirs or successors, with any customs, subsidies, or licenses of any tin issuing out of this our Kingdom of England, unless only as other merchants in the same county may be charged, &c., towards us, or have been towards our progenitors, in time of which memory is not, within our ports of London and Southampton, for any customs, subsidies, or licenses of tin issuing Out of this our Kingdom of England; but we will, &c., that the aforesaid Robert, John, &c., and every of them, merchants of tin, and all other buyers, venders, &c. shall be exonerated, &c., by these presents, from all new impositions, &c., so that the said Robert, John, &c., shall not hereafter be charged in any manner for any customs, &c., of tin out of this our kingdom of England, unless as other native buyers, venders, and merchants are charged, or any native merchant is or hath been charged, towards us and our progenitors, within our said ports of London and Southampton aforesaid; and further, that all pardons, &c., by us pardoned, &c., to the aforesaid Robert, John, &c., and to all other offenders or offender, breakers or breaker, of any statutes, ordinances, proclamations, or provisions, made, edited, or ordained by us or our progenitors, &c., touching any tinners, bounders,

125

possessors, blowers, workers, buyers, venders, merchants of tin, or any other meddling with tin as aforesaid, may and shall be in our next Parliament, &c., authorised; and that all grants by us granted, and all annullings of all statutes, acts, &c., aforesaid, by our grants aforesaid annulled, at the petition and request of the said Robert, John, &c., shall be confirmed in the said Parliament, that as well the same Robert, John, &c., may enjoy all our said grants and annullings, so that all statutes, &c., before made, shall be revoked, annulled, and made void, according to the advice and council of the advisers or adviser of the aforesaid Robert, John, &c., to their best profit and greatest advantage as to them shall seem best to be done, &c.

And further, &c., we have granted, &c., to the aforesaid Robert, John, &c., that no supervision of our customs and subsidies in our County of Cornwall aforesaid, nor any searcher of the same customs and subsidies in the said county, from henceforth and hereafter, shall take for the weighing of any tin issuing out of this our kingdom of England, for his fee, by reason of the weighing of the same tin, so issuing out of our kingdom of England aforesaid, only the same as is given to him, and to all other weighers, by a certain statute, edited in the Parliament of the Lord Edward, late King of England the Third, our progenitor, holden in the fourteenth year of his reign, (that is to say) for every weight of forty pounds, one farthing; and from the weight of forty pounds unto the weight of one hundred pounds, one halfpenny; and for every weight of one hundred pounds, unto the weight of a thousand pounds, one penny, and no more, as in the said statute more fully appears.

And further, we grant that every weighers of tin, in our town of Southampton, for the time being, shall take from every merchant of tin in our County of Cornwall, for the weighing of his tin, brought or hereafter to be brought into our town of

Southampton, the same as is given to him by the said statute, and no more.

In witness whereof &c., Witness the King at Westminster, the twelfth day of July, in the twenty-third year of the reign of King Henry the Seventh. By writ of privy-seal, and of the date, &c.

Resolution of the Judges in 1608[267]

The Resolution of all the Judges by force of his Majestyes letters concernyng the stannaries in Devon and Cornwall, upon the hearing of the Councell learned of both partyes at severall dayes and what could be alledged and shewed on either party and upon viewe and hearing of the former proceedings in the Courts of the Stannarie, both before and since a certaine Act of Parliament made concernyng the Stannaries in quin-quagesimo Edwardi tercii vicesimo sexto Novembris, millesimo sexcentesimo octavo at Serjeants Inne.

First we are of opynion that as well Blowers as all other Laborers and workers without fraud or covyn in or about the Stannaries in Cornwall and Devon are to have the priviledge of the Stannaries duryng the tyme that they doe worke there. Secondly, that all matters and things concernyng the Stannaries or depending upon the same are to be heard and determyned in those Courts according to the custome of the same, tyme out of mynd of man used. Thirdly, that all transitory accions betweene Tynner and Tynner or worker and worker (though the case be collaterall and not perteyning to the Stannarie) maye be heard and determyned within the Courts of the Stannaries according to the Custome of the said Courts, albeit the cause of accion did rise in any place out of the Stannaries, if the defendant be found within the Stannarie, or may be sued at the Common Lawe at the election of the Plaintife, but if the one party only be a tynner or worker, and the cause of accion being transitorye and collateral to the

---

267 Lewis, G. R *The Stannaries—A Study of the Medieval Tin Miners of Cornwall and Devon* (1908) p 245

stannarie doe rise out of the said stannaries, then the Defendant maye by the custome and usage of those courts plead to the jurisdiccion of the Court that the cause of accion did rise out of the Stannaries and the Jurisdiccion of those courts which by the custome of the Court he ought to plead in proper person upon oath. And if such plea to the Jurisdiccion be not allowed, then a prohibicion in that case is to be graunted, and if in that case the defendant doe come to pleade to the Jurisdiccion of the Court upon his oath, he ought not to be arrested eundo redeundo vel morando, at the suite of any subject, in anye Corporacion or other place where the said Courts of the Stannerie shalbe then holden.

Fourthly, if the Defendant maye plead to the Jurisdiccion of the Court in the case before mencioned and will not but plead and admitt the Jurisdiccion of the Court and Judgment is given and the body of the defendant taken in execucion, the Party cannot by Lawe have any accion of false imprisonment, but the execucion is good by the custome of that Court; but if in that case it doth appeare by the Plaintife's owne shewing that the contract or cause of accion was made or did rise out of the Stanneries and the Jurisdiccion of those Courts or if it appeare by the condicion of the bond whereupon the accion is grounded that the condicion was to be performed in any place out of the Jurisdiccion of those Courts then all the proceedings in such cases upon such matter apparant are coram non Judice.

Fifthly, We are of opynion that noe man ought to demurre in that Court for want of forme, but only for substance of matter, as if an accion be brought there for words which will beare no accion or an accion of debt upon a contract against executors or admynistrators or such like. In such cases a Demurrer maye be upon the matter and that the proceedings there must be according to the custome of those courtes used tyme out of mynd of man for that noe writt of error doth lye upon any Judgment given there but the remedy given to the party grieved is by appeale as hath byn tyme out of mynd of man accustomed.

Sixthly, that the Courts of the Stannary have not any Jurisdiccion for any cause of accion that is locall rising out of the stannary.

Seventhlv, that the Priviledge of the workers in the Stannaries do not extend to any cause of accion that is locall rising out of the Stannaries nor for any cause locall rising within the Stannaries whereby any Freehold shall bedemaunded, for that makers of life, member, and Plea of Land are excepted by expresse words in their charters and noe man can be ex empt from Justice.

Thos: Fleming. Edw: Coke.

Close Roll, 6 James I, pt. v.

Resolutions of the Privy Council, 1632[268]

(Order of January 2 1632.)

Whereas an humble peticion was heretofore presented to his Majestie by the Earle of Pembroke and Montgomery, Lord Warden of the Stanaryes concerning the jurisdiccion and priviledges of the said Staneries and by his command sent to the Lords Cheife Justices of both Benches with the rest of his Majesties justices there, to be by them pervsed, and considered, to the end some course might be setled for the distinguishing, regulateing and ordering of the limitts and priviledges of the seuerall Jurisdiccions of the said Courts, that his Majesties Subjects might the better know whether they were to resort for the Administracion of Justice, and the heareing of their causes, and righting of their wrongs. Upon a long heareing and debate of this business (his Majestie then sitting in Councell) and the said Judges being present, as also his Majesties Atturney generall. It was resolued, and ordered that the said Judges should search out and peruse such Statutes, and other Records as might concerne that business And also that Mr. Atturney should doe the like, and conferr with the said judges for the cleareing of the jurisdiccion of the said Staneries, that so if they could not reconsile and accommodate the differences aforesaid among themselues, then before, or at the longest on the 18th of February next, they should attend his Majestie and make Report of the state of the cause, to the end that his Majestie

---

268 Lewis, G. R *The Stannaries—A Study of the Medieval Tin Miners of Cornwall and Devon* (1908) p 249

may thereupon settle such a final conclusion therein, as in his princely wisdome shall be fitt.

(February 18, 1632)

This day (his Majestie being present in Councell) certaine Articles and Proposicions produced by his Majesties Attorney generall concerning the Jurisdiction of the Stannaries, were read and approued of by the Board; only some fewe particulars thought fitt to be added were by his Majestie recomended to his said Attorny generall; who is likewise required to cause a faire transcript thereof to be signed by the Judges, before they goe theire Circuite and to retourne the same to this Board, to the end it may be kept in the Councell chest.

The Rules following to be observed in his Majesties Courts at Westminster and his Court of the Stanneries were agreed of before the Board, his Majestie being present in Councell and afterwards subsigned by the Lord Warden of the Stanneries and all the Judges of his Majesties said Courts at Westminster and his Atturney Generall. And the Transcript thereof ordered to be entered into the Register of Councell Causes and the originall to remayne in the Councell chest.

The Workers about the Tynne, whether in Myne or Streame. the Carrier, Washer, and Blower of Tynne, and the necessarie Attendants aboute the workes have priviledge that they ought not to be sued out of the Stannery (except it be in causes concerning Life, Member, or Freehould) for any cause aryseinig within the Stannerie. And if they be sued elsewhere the warden may demand Conusans or the partie may plead his priviledge.

Besides theise there are other Tynriers that doe noe handworke as are the owners of the Soyle, owners of the Bounds, owners of the Bloweing houses, and theire partners, buyers and sellers of Black Tynne, or Whyte Tynne before the deliuerance, theise may sue one an other, or working Tynners, or any other man, for any matter concerning Tynne, or Tynne works, in the Stannerie Courte.

Both theise Tynners and the workers may sue one an other in the Stannarye for all causes personall not concerning Freehold, Life or Mem ber, ariscing within the Stannary or elsewhere aryseing.

One Tynner may sue a Forrayner in all lyke causes personall, aryseing within the Stannarye, but a Tynner may not sue a Forrayner, in the Stannarye for matters personall aryseing out of the Stannarye.

Of those later sorte of Tynners, such onely are intended as within some convenient tyme, make profitt or endeavour to make profitt to the Coynage.

For the manner of tryeing whether one be a Tynner or not, the use in Cornewall is by Plea, and if issue be joyned, and found for the Plaintiffe it is not peremptory but a respondes.

In Devon it is by the oath of the partye.

For the Extent of the Stannaries.
We cannot yet discerne but that the Stannaries doe extend over the whole County of Cornwall.

In Devon there hath bin long Question concerning the extent of the Stannarie, as apeareth in sunderie Peticions in Parliament.

This is question of Fact and not of Lawe.

But for repose and quiettnes hereafter, whether it be convenient to award a Commission to some able persons who may enquire by oath of lawfull and indifferent men of the Bounds of each Stannarve for informacion onely, or whether it be more fitt to leave it without further enquirie and as it bath byn heretofore wee humbly leave it to your Majesties wisedome, with this; that untill the matter of fact be further knowne, this Question concerning the Bounds of the Stannarye in the County of Devon may remayne without prejudice, by occacion of any former opinion delivered concerning this question of facte. But

The exempcion of Tynners from Toll is over the whole county.

The power to digg and search for Tvnne is over the whole county saueing under houses, orchards, gardens, etc.

The Tynne wrought in any parte of the county must be brought to the Coynage.

The priviledge of Empcion or preempcion is of Tynne gotten over the whole county.

Judgernents had in the Stannarye Courte are Leaviable in all parts of the county.

Fynes and Amerciaments sett in the Stannary Courte may be leavied over the whole county by Proces of the Stannarie.

For trespasses in Tynne works, Proces may be executed in the whole county.

Water Courses for the Tynne works on Tynne Mills may be made in any place of the countye.

Register of the Privy Council, Charles 1, vol. 8, pp. 412, 457, 485, 486. (Printed with omissions in Harrison's Report on the Jurisdiction of the Stannaries, pp. 158—160)

Appendix II

Warrant for Commission for holding a Convocation of Tinners[269]

"Charles, Duke of Cornwall To Our right trusty, &c., Sir Nicholas Bacon, Warden of our Stannaries, greeting, Whereas divers and sundry things are at this time very requisite to be redressed and provided for within Our stannaries of Cornwall and Devon, by which the privileges and liberties of Our said stannaries heretofore granted by Our royal predecessors, kings and queens of this realm, unto the tinners of the said respective stannaries, ought, as in like cases have always heretofore been used and accustomed, to be amended, redressed, and provided for, by and with the consent of a convocation or parliament of tinners for the stannaries in the said respective counties to be summoned by virtue of letters under the privy seal to the warden of the stannaries for the time being directed, and not otherwise. We, therefore, not minding to break or take away

---

269 Manning, J. and Ryland, A., *Report of Cases Argued and determined in the Court of King's Bench Volume III* (1830) p 497

the liberties, privileges, and customs of Our said stannaries, but to establish, augment, and confirm the same, and also to have the same from henceforth used, executed, and continued, in as large and ample manner as they have been heretofore: Do require and demand you, by virtue of, &c'

Appendix III

**Charter to the Community of the Land of Cornwall
(Charter Roll 45 Hen. III No 11 18th June 1261)**

Sea-Sand (Devon and Cornwall) Act 1609

Charter to the Community
of the Land of Cornwall

(Charter Roll 45 Hen. III No 11
18th June A.D. 1261)

The King to the Archbishops, etc greeting. Whereas, our vey dear brother Richard, the illustrous King of the Romans, ever august, for the common advantage of the whole land of Cornwall, did grant for himself and his heirs, that for all and every the inhabitants of the same land may have and take in all lands of him, the said King, and of his men, and also throughout all Cornwall, sea sand without payment; and throughout the lands of him, the said King, and of his men, throughout all Cornwall, may freely, peaceably, and without let of any one be able to heap up (or stack) the sand upon their lands and to carry it throughout all Cornwall, by a reasonable way (or road) assigned or to be assigned to them, for the fertilization of the same land. So, nevertheless, that if the same King, or they over whose lands or upon whose lands it shall happen that the aforesaid sand be carried or stacked, shall incur any damage, on account of the stacking or way, a competent satisfaction shall be made to them in reasonable compensation of such damage, to be taxed upon the award of good and lawful men of the same land, and by the Steward for the time being of him the said King; or an agreement may be made with them beforehand for a sum certain, as in the Charter of the aforesaid King thereupon to the community of the land aforesaid, and which we have inspected, more fully it is contained. We ratfying and approving the said grant, do grant and confirm the same, so far as to us pertains, for us and our heirs, as the Charter aforesaid to him the said King, our brother, doth reasonably testify. These being witnesses: William de Valence, our brother Reghinald Fitz Peter, and others etc. Given under the hand of Master Nicholas, Archdeacon of Ely, our Chancellor, at Guildford, on the 18th day of June.

SEA-SAND (DEVON AND CORNWALL) ACT 1609

AN Acte for the takinge landinge and carryinge of Sea Sand for the bettringe of Ground and for the Increase of Corne and Tillage within the Counties of Devon and Cornwall

WHEREAS the Sea Sand by longe triall and experience hath beene found to be very pfitable for the bettring of Land, and espially for the increase of Corne and Tillage within the Counties of Devon and Cornwall, where most parte of the Inhabitants have not comonly used any other Worth, for the bettringe of their Arrable Ground and Pastures; nowithstanding dyvers having Landes adjoyning to the Sea Coast there, have of late intrupted the Bargemen and sduch others as have used at their free will and pleasure to fetch the said Seasand to take the same under the full Seamarke as they have heretofore used to doe, unlesse they make Composicion with them at such Rates as they themselves sett downe, though they have smal or no damage to losse thereby, to the greart Decay and Hinderaunce of Husbandry and Tillage within the said Counties: Be it therefore enacted by the King's most Excellent Majestie, the Lords Spiritual and Temporall and the Comons in thisd present Parliament assembled and by the Authoritie of the same, That it shall and may be lawful to and for all persons whatsoever, resiant and dwelling withinn the said Couties of Devon and Cornwall, to fetch and takle Seasand at all Places under the full seamarke, where the same shalbe cast by the Sea, for the bettring of their Land, and for the the increase of Corne and Tillage, at their willes and pleasures: And that itg shall and may be alsoe lawfull to and for all Bargemen and Boatemen, and all other Carriers of Seasand of the said Counties, that shall fetch or take Sand as aforesaid, to land and cast out their Boates and Barges such Sand as they shall soe fetch or take, to such Places as Sand hath at anty tyme within the Space of fiftie yeeres last past beene used by such Bargemen or Boatmen to be landed and cast, and also to fetch and carrie gthe same by and thorough such Wayes as now be and by the Space of Twentie yeers last past, have beene used for the carryage and fetching thereof, paying for the taking casting out and landing of every Bargeloade Boateloade or Sack of the said Sanbd, upon Groundes of any Man, such Duties as heretofore within the said tyme of Fiftie yeeres have beene used and accustomed to be paid for the same, and for passage by and thgorough the said Waies, such Duties as have usually beene paid by the Space of Twentie yeeres, and in such manner and forme as the same within ther said severall tymes have respectively bene used and accustomed to be paid; And in such places where certain usual Duties have not bene paid, but uincertain Composicions have from tyme to tyme bene made by Agreemeant with the Owners of the Soyle there, to yeeld such reasonable Comnposicions as by Agreement with the said Owners, shall from tyme to tyme be made.

Appendix IV

CHARTERS OF THE DUCHY OF CORNWALL

Charter Edward III (17th March 1337)
    The Duchy of Cornwall (The Great Charter)

Charter Edward III (18th March 1337)

Charter Edward III (3rd January 1338)

The Fordington Charter Edward III (9th July 1343)

Inspeximus Charter of King Henry VII
    (30th April 1488)

CHARTER
11 Edward III
(also known as the Great Charter of Creation of the Duchy of Cornwall)[270]

(17th March 1337)

For Edward, Duke of Cornwall

Edward by the grace of God, King of England, Lord of Ireland and Duke of Aquitaine, To his archbishops, bishops, abbots, priors, earls, barons, justices, sheriffs reeves, ministers, and all bailiffs and lieges, greeting: Amongst the glories of royalty We esteem this the chiefest, that it be fortified by a suitable distribution of orders, dignities, and offices, supported by sound counsels, and upheld by the strength of the brave; and inasmuch as many hereditary titles in Our kingdom, as well by the descent of inheritances, according to the law of this kingdom, to co-heirs and parceners, as also by default of issue, and by various events have come to Our royal hands, whereby Our said kingdom hath long time suffered great deficiency in names, and honors, and in the dignity of ranks, We therefore earnestly meditating those things whereby Our kingdom may be adorned, and whereby Our said kingdom and the holy church thereof, and the other lands subject to Our dominion, may be more securely and honourably defended against the attempts of their enemies and adversaries, and desiring to dignify the chief places of Our kingdom with their ancient

270 Manning, J., *Reports of cases argued and determined in the Court of Kings Bench during Michaelmas Term Ninth Geo IV* (1830) p 474-482

honour, and turning Our attention closely to the person of Our well beloved and faithful Edward, Earl of Chester, Our first begotten son, and We wishing to honour the person of Our said son, have, with the common consent and counsel of the prelates, earls, barons, and others of Our council in this Our present Parliament at Westminster, upon Monday next after the Feast of St. Matthias the Apostle last past, being assembled, given to Our said son the name and honour of Duke of Cornwall, and have constituted him Duke of Cornwall, and girt him with a sword, as behoveth. And that there may be no doubt hereafter, what, or how much the same duke, or other dukes of the same place for the time being, under the name of the said dukedom ought to have, Our will is, that all in specialty which to the said dukedom doth belong be inserted in this Our charter. Therefore, for Us and Our heirs, We have given and granted, and by this Our charter confirmed to Our said son, under the name and honour of duke of the said place, the castles, manors, lands, tenements, and other things under written, that he the state and honour of such duke may uphold according to the nobility of his race, and the charges and burthens thereof the better to support, that is to say: The shrievalty of Cornwall, with the appurtenances, so as the said duke, and other dukes of the same place for the time being, do make, constitute, and appoint sheriffs of the said county of Cornwall at their will and pleasure and to do and execute the office of sheriffs there as heretofore it used to be done, without any hindrance of Us or Our heirs for ever; as also the castle, borough, manor, and honour of Launceneton , With the park there, and other its appurtenances in the counties of Cornwall and Devon; the castle and manor of Tremeton, with the town of Saltesh, and the park there, and other its appurtenances in the said counties; the castle, borough, and manor of Tyntagell, with the appurtenances in the said county of Cornwall; the castle and manor of Restormel, with the park there, and other its appurtenances in the same county; and the manor of Clymmeslond, with the park of Kerribullok,and other its appurtenances; Tybeste, with the bailiwick of Poudershire, and other its appurtenances; Tewynton, with the appurtenances; Helleston in Kerrier, with the appurtenances; Moresk, with the appurtenances; Tewernaill, with the appurtenances; Pengkneth, with the appurtenances; Penlyn, with the park there, and other its appurtenances; Rellaton, with the bedelry of Estwyneleshire, and other its appurtenances; Helleston, in Trygsbire, with the park of Hellesbury, and other its appurtenances; Lyskeret, with the park there, and other its appurtenances; Calystock, with the fishery there, and other its appurtenances; and Talskydy, with the appurtenances, in the same county of Cornwall; and the town of Lostwithiell in the same county, with the mills there, and other its appurtenances; and Our prizage and customs of wines in the said county of Cornwall; and also all the profits of Our ports, within the same county of Cornwall to us belonging together with wreck of the sea as well of whales and sturgeon other fishes which do belong to Us by reason of our prerogative as whatsoever other things belong to such wreck of the sea, with the appurtenances in all Our said county of Cornwall; and the profits and emoluments to Us belonging, of Our county Courts holden in Our county of Cornwall, and of hundreds and Courts thereof in the said county; as also Our Stannary in the said county of Cornwall. together with the coinage of the said Stannary and all issues and profits thereof arising; and also the explees, profits, and perquisites of the Court of Stannary, and the mines of the said county, except only 1000 marks, which to Our beloved and faithful William dc Monte-Acuto, Earl of Salisbury, We have granted, for Us and Our heirs, to be taken to him, and the heirs male of his body lawfully begotten, of the issues and profits of the aforesaid coinage, until there should come to his or their hands the castle and manor of Tonbridge, with the appurtenances in the county of Wilts, and the manors of Aldeburn, Ambresbury, and Winterbourn, with the appurtenances in the said county, and the manor of Caneford, with the appurtenances in the county of Dorset, and the manors of Henstrig and Charleton, with the appurtenances in the county of Somerset, which Our beloved and faithful John de Warren, Earl of Surrey, and Joan his wife, hold for the term of their lives, and which after their deaths to Us and Our heirs ought to revert, the remainder whereof We have granted, after the decease of the said Earl and Joan, to the aforesaid Earl of Salisbury and the heirs male of his body lawfully begotten, to the value of 800 marks by the year, and also of lands and rents of the value of 200 marks, which to the said Earl of Salisbury to have in form aforesaid, we granted to provide; and also our Stannary in the aforesaid county of Devon with the coinage and all issues and profits of and The issues, profits, and perquisites of the said Court of Stannary, and the water of Dartmouth in the said county, and the yearly farm of £20 of Our city of Exeter and Our prizage and customs of wines, in the water of Sutton in the said county of Devon, as also the castle of Walyngford, with its hamlets and members, and the yearly farm of the town of Walyngford, with the honour, of Walyngford and Saint Vallery, with the appurtenances in the county of Oxford, and other counties wheresoever those honour. may be, and the castle, manor, and town of Berkham-stead, with the park there, together with the honour of Berkhamstead in the counties of Hertford, Buckingham, and Northampton, and other their appurtenances, and the manor of Byflet with the park there, and other it. appurtenances; in the County of Surry: To have and to hold to the said Duke and to the first begotten sons of him and his Kings of England being dukes of the said place and heirs apparent to the said kingdom of England; together with the knights fees and advowson of churches, abbeys, priories, hospitals, and chapels, and with the hundreds, fisheries, forests, chases, parks, woods, warrens, fairs, markets, liberties, free customs, wards, reliefs, escheats, and services of tenants, as well free as villein, and all other things to the aforesaid castles, boroughs, towns, manor, honors, Stannaries and coinages, lands and tenements, howsoever and wheresoever be longing or appertaining, of Us and Our heirs for ever, together with 24*l.* of yearly farm, which Our beloved and faithful John de Meere to Us by the year for all his life is bound to pay for the castle and manor of Meere, with the appurtenances, in the county of Wilts, granted to him by Us for the term of his life, to be taken every year by the hands of the said John for the term of his life, and with the aforesaid 1000 marks yearly to the aforesaid Earl of Surrey of the issues of the coinage aforesaid by Us so granted after seisin obtained by him or his heirs males of his body begotten of the said castle and manor of Tunbridge, and the manors of Aldebourn, Ambresbury, Winterbourn, Caneford, Hengstiigg, and Carleton, after the deaths of the said Earl of Surrey and Joan, and of the land. and rents of the value of 200 marks to the said Earl of Salisbury and the heir. males of his body begotten, so to be provided as an equivalent for their portion of the said castle, manor, land, and tenements, when they shall wholly or partially come to the hands of the said Earl of Salisbury or of the heirs males of his body. We have moreover granted for Us and Our heirs, and by this Our charter We have confirmed, That the castle and manor of Knaresburgh with the hamlets and members thereof and the honour of Knaresburgh, in the county of York, and other counties, wheresoever the same honour may be, the manor of lstilworth, with the appurtenances, in the county of Middlesex, which Philippa, Queen of England, Our most dear consort, holds for term of life, and the castle and manor of Lydeford, with the appurtenances and with the chase of Dertmore, with the appurtenances, in the said county of Devon, and the manor of Bradenesh, with the

147

appurtenances, in the same county, which Our beloved and faithful Hugh d'Audele, Earl of Gloucester, and Margaret his wife hold for the life of the said Margaret; and the said castle and manor of Meere, with the appurtenances, which the aforesaid Joan so for life holdeth of Our grant, and which after the death of the said Queen, Margaret and John, to Us and Our heirs ought to revert, that is to say, after the decease of the said Queen, the castle and manor of Knaresburgh, with the honor, hamlets and member, thereof aforesaid, and other its appurtenances, and the manor of Istilworth, with the appurtenances, and after the death of the said Margaret, the said castle and manor of Lydeford with the said chase of Dertmore and other its appurtenances, and the manor of Bradeneshe, with the appurtenances, and after the death of the said John, the said castle and manor of Meere, with the appurtenances, shall remain to the aforesaid duke and to the first begotten sons of him and his heirs, kings of England, being Dukes of the said place and heirs apparent to the kingdom of England, as before is said To have and to hold together with the said knights' fees, advowsons of churches, abbeys, priories, hospitals, and chapels, with hundreds, wapentakes, fisheries, forests, chases, parks, woods, warrens, fairs, markets, liberties, free customs, wards, reliefs, escheats, services of tenants, as well free as villein, and all other things to the same castles, manors, and honour, howsoever and wheresover belonging, or appertaining of Us likewise and Our heirs for ever, all which castles, boroughs, towns, manors, honor, Stannaries, coinages, rents (*firmas*) of Exeter and Wallingford, lands and tenements as above are specified, together with the fees, advowsons, and all other things afore said, to the aforesaid duchy, by Our present charter, for Us and Our heirs We do annex and unite to the same for ever to remain, so that from the said duchy at no time they be any ways severed nor to any person or persons other than dukes of the same place, by Us or Our heirs be given, or in any manner granted; so also, as that whenever the abovesaid duke or other dukes of the same place shall depart this life, and a son or sons to whom the said duchy, by virtue of Our grants aforesaid, is appointed to belong shall not then appear, the said duchy, with the castles, boroughs, towns, and other the abovesaid to Us, Our heirs, kings of England, shall revert, to be retained in Our hands and in the hands of our heir, kings of England, until such son or sons, being heir or heirs apparent to the said kingdom of England, shall appear, as before is said, to whom then successively We, for Us and Our heirs, grant and will that the said duchy with the appurtenances be delivered, to hold, as above is expressed; We have moreover for Us and Our heirs granted, and by this Our charter confirmed, to the aforesaid duke, that the said duke and such first begotten sons of him and of his heirs, dukes of the same place, shall for ever have free warren in all the demesne lands of the castles, lands, and other places aforesaid, so as the said lands be not within the bounds of Our forest; so that none enter into them to hunt in them or to take any thing which to warren appertaineth without the licence and will of the said duke or other dukes of the same place, under forfeiture to Us of *10l.* Wherefore We will and firmly command for Us and Our heirs, that the said duke have and hold to him and the first begotten sans of him and his heirs kings of England, being Dukes of the same place and heirs apparent to the said kingdom of England, the said shrievalty of Cornwall, with the appurtenances, so that they and the other dukes aforesaid, at their wills make and constitute the sheriff of the said county of Cornwall, to do and execute the office of a sheriff there as hither to it used to be done, without the hindrance of Us or Our heirs for ever. Also the said castle, borough, manor, and honour of Launceston; castle and manor of Tremeton, with the town of Saltesh; castle, borough, and manor of Tyntagel; castle and manor of Rostormel, also the manors of

Clymmesland, Tybeste, Tewynton, Helleston in Kerier, Moresk, Tewarnaill, Pengkueth, Penlyn, Rellaton, Helleston in Trygshire, Lyskeret, Calistok, Talskydy, and the town of Lostwythiell, with the appurtenances, together with the park, bailiwick, bedelry, fisheries, and other things abovesaid, in the aforesaid county of Cornwall, and the aforesaid prisages, customs, and profits of ports aforesaid, together with the said wreck of the sea and the said profits and emoluments of the counties, hundreds, and Courts to Us belonging, and the said Stannary in the said county of Cornwall, together with the coinage of the said Stannary, and with all issues and profits thereof arising, and also the explees, profits, and perquisites of the Courts aforesaid (except only the said 1000 marks, which to Our well-beloved and faithful William de Monte-acuto, Earl of Salisbury, We granted, for Us and Our heirs to be taken to him and the heirs males of his body Lawfully begotten, of the issues and profits of the coinage aforesaid, until to his or their hands the said castle and manor of Tonbrigg, with the appurtenances, and the said manors of Aldebourn, Ambres-bury, and Winterbourn, with the appurtenances, and the said manor of Hengstrygg and Charlton, with the appurtenances, which the aforesaid Earl of Surry and Joan his wife hold for the term of their lives, and which after their deaths to Us and Our heirs ought to revert, the remainder whereof, after the deceases of the said Earl and Joan, We granted to the said Earl of Salisbury and the heirs males of his body lawfully begotten, to the value of 800 marks by the year, and the lands and rents of the value of 200 marks, which to the said Earl of Salisbury to have in form aforesaid We granted, shall come, as before is said;) and the said Stannary in the county of Devon, with the coinage and all issues and profits thereof, and also the explees, profits, and perquisites of the Court of the same Stannary, the water of Dertmouth, and the said yearly farm of *20l* of the said city of Exeter,… the said prizage and custom of wines in the water of Sutton, in the county of Devon, as also the aforesaid castle of Walyngford, with its hamlets and members, the yearly farm of the town of Walyngford, with the said honours of Walyngford and St. Valery, the castle, manor, and town of Berkhampsted, with the said honour of Berkhampsted, and the manor of Byflete, with its parks and other appurtenances as aforesaid, together with knights' fees, advowsons of churches, abbeys, priories, hospitals and chapels, and with the hundreds, fisheries, forests, chases, parks, woods, warrens, fairs, markets, liberties, free customs, wards, reliefs, escheats, and services of tenants, as well free as villein, and all other things to the said castles, boroughs, towns, manors, honors, Stannaries and coinages, lands, and tenements, whatsoever and wheresoever, belonging or appertaining, of Us and Our heirs for ever, together with the said *24l* of annual farm which the aforesaid John de Meere to us yearly for his whole life is bound to pay for the said castle and manor of Meere, granted to him by Us to bold for the term of his life, to be taken yearly by the hands of the said John de Meere all his life, and also with the aforesaid 1000 annual marks to the aforesaid Earl of Salisbury of the profits of the coinage aforesaid by Us so granted, after seisin shall have been obtained by him or the heirs males of his body be gotten, as well of the aforesaid manor of Tonbrigg and manors of Aldebourn, Ambresbury, Winterbourn, Caneford, Hengstrigg, and Charlton, after the decease of the said Earl of Surry and Joan, as also of the said land and rent of the value of 200 marks to the said Earl of Salisbury and the said heirs males of his body, so to be provided as an equivalent for their portion of the said castle, manors, lands, and tenements, when the estate wholly or partially come to the hands of the said Earl of Salisbury, or the heirs males of his body lawfully begotten, as aforesaid; and that the aforesaid castle and manor of Knaresburgh, with its hamlets and members and with the honour of Knaresburgh and the manor of lstilworth, with the

151

appurtenances, after the death of Our aforesaid consort; the castle and manor of Lydeford, with the appurtenances, and with the said chase of Dertmore, with the appurtenances, and the manor of Bradnesh, with the appurtenances, after the decease of the aforesaid Margaret; and the castle and manor of Meere, with their appurtenances, after the death of the aforesaid John de Meere, shall remain to the said duke, to have and to hold, to him and to the first begotten sons of him and his heirs, kings of England, being dukes of the same place, and heirs apparent to the said kingdom, together with knights' fees and advowsons of churches, abbeys, priories, hospitals, and chapels, and with hundreds, wapentakes, fisheries forests, chases, parks, woods, warrens, fairs, markets, liberties, free customs, wards, reliefs, escheats, and services of tenants, as well free as villein, and all other things to the said castles, manors, and honours, howsoever and wheresoever belonging and appertaining, of Us likewise, and Our heirs for ever, as before is said. All which castles, boroughs, towns, manors, and honours, Stannaries, and coinages, rents (*firmas*) of Exeter and Walyngford, lands and tenements, as above are specified, together with the knights' fees, advowsons, all other things above said, to the said duchy by this Our present charter, for Us and Our heirs, We do annex and unite to the same, to remain for ever, so as from the said duchy at no time hereafter they be severed, nor to any person or persons than the dukes of the same place by Us or Our heirs they be given, or in any ways granted, so, also, as that whenever the said duke, or other dukes of the same place, shall depart this life, and a son or sons to whom the said duchy by virtue of our said grants is appointed to belong, shall not then appear, the same duchy, with the castles, boroughs, towns, and all other things aforesaid, to Us, and Our heirs,. kings of England, shall revert, to be retained in our hands, and in the hands of Our heirs, kings of England, until such son or sons, heir or heirs apparent to the said kingdom of England, shall appear, as before is said, to whom then successively, We, for Us and Our heirs, grant and will that the said duchy, with the appurtenances, be delivered to be holden, as above is expressed; and that the said duke, and the first begotten son of him and of his heirs, dukes of the said place, for ever, have free warren in all the demesne lands aforesaid, so that the same lands be not within the bounds of Our forest, so as that none enter into those lands to hunt in them, or to take any thing which to warren belongeth, without the licence and will of the said duke and the other dukes of the said place, under forfeiture to Us of £10, as before is said.

Witnesses, the venerable John, Archbishop of Canterbury, Primate of all England, Our chancellor; Henry, Bishop of Lincoln, Our treasurer; Richard, Bishop of Durham; John de Warren, Earl of Surrey; Thomas de Bello Campo, Earl of Warwick; Thomas Wake, of Lydell; and John de Mowbray; John Darcy, Le Neveu, steward of Our household, and others. Given by Our hand, at Westminster, the 17th day of March, in the eleventh year of Our reign,

By the king himself and all the council in Parliament

Charter
11 Edward III

(18th March 1337)

Edward, by the grace of God, King of England, Lord of Ireland, and Duke of Aquitaine, to his archbishops, bishops, abbots, priors, earls, barons, justices, sheriffs, reeves, ministers, and all his bailiffs, and lieges, greeting. Know, that whereas We lately willing to honour the person of Our faithful and beloved Edward, Earl of Chester, Our first begotten son, did, by the common assent and counsel of the prelates, earls, barons, and others of Our council, (being called together in Our present Parliament at Westminster, on Monday next after the feast of St. Matthias the Apostle last past,) give to Our said son the name and honour of duke of Cornwall, and appointed him to be duke of Cornwall, and girded him with a sword, as it behoved; and that he the state and honour of a duke might be able to maintain in a manner becoming the nobility of his race, and to support his charges in that behalf, We did give and grant by Our charter, for Us and Our heirs, to Our said son, under the name and honour of duke of the said place, the shrievalty of Cornwall, with the appurtenances; also the castle, borough, manor, and honour, of Launceneton, with the parks there, and other its appurtenances in the counties of Cornwall and Devon; the castle and manor of Tremeton, with the town of Saltesh, and the park there, and other its appurtenances In the counties aforesaid, the castle, borough, and manor of Tyntagell, with the appurtenances in the said county of Cornwall; the castle and manor of Rostormell, with the park

---

271 Manning, J., *Reports of cases argued and determined in the Court of Kings Bench during Michaelmas Term Ninth Geo IV* (1830) p 482-485

there, and other its appurtenances in the same county, also the manors of Clymmeslond, with the park of Kerribullok, and others its appurtenances, Tybest, with the bailiwick of Poudershire, and other its appurtenances, Tcwynton, with the appurtenances, Helleston, in Kerrier, with the appurtenances, Moresk, with the appurtenances, Tewernail, with the appurtenances, Pengkneth, with the appurtenances, Penlyn, with the park there, and other its appurtenances, Rellaton, with the bedelry of Estwynelshire, and other its appurtenances, Helleston, in Tregshire, with the park of Hellesby, and other its appurtenances, Lyskeret, with the park there, and other its appurtenances, Calystok, with the fishery there, and other its appurtenances, Talskydy, with the appurtenances in the same county of Cornwall, and the town of Lostwithiel, in the same county, with the mills there, and other its appurtenances; and Our prizage and customs of wines in the said county of Cornwall; also all profits of Our ports within the said county of Cornwall to Us belonging, together with wreck of the sea, as well of whale and sturgeon and other fishes, which belong to Us by reason of Our prerogative, as also of all other things to wreck of the sea in what manner soever belonging, in all the aforesaid county of Cornwall; also the profits and emoluments to Us be longing of county Courts (*comitatuum*) held in the said county of Cornwall, and of hundreds and hundred Courts in that county; also Our Stannaries in the said county of Cornwall, and together with the coinage of the said Stannaries, and with all issues and profits arising therefrom, and the explees, profits, and perquisites of Courts of Stannary and mines in the said county, except only 1000 marks, which We had granted to Our faithful and beloved William de Monte-Acuto, Earl of Sarum, to be received by him and his heirs males of his body lawfully begotten; of the issues and profits of the coinage aforesaid in a certain form, more fully described in Our other charter, to the said duke thereof made, to have and to hold to the said duke, and to the first begotten sons of himself and of his heirs, Kings of England, being dukes of the said place and heirs apparent to the said kingdom of England, together with knights fees and advowsons of churches, abbeys, priories, hospitals, and chapels, and with the hundreds, fisheries, forests, chases, parks, woods, warrens, fairs, markets, liberties, free customs, wards, reliefs, escheats and services of tenants, as well free as bondsmen; and all other things to the said castles, town, manors, honors, Stannaries, coinages, lands, and tenements, howsoever and wheresoever belonging or appertaining, together with certain other manors, lands, and tenements, in divers other counties of Our kingdom, of Us and Our heirs for ever, as in the said other charter is more fully contained: We, willing to do more ample favour to the said duke in this behalf for the support of such honour, have granted for Us and Our heirs, that the said duke, and the first begotten sons of him and his heirs kings of England being dukes of the same place, and heirs apparent to the said kingdom of England, do for ever have the return of all writs of Us and Our heirs, and of summonses of the Exchequer of Us and Our heirs, and attachments, as well in pleas of the crown as in all others, in all his said lands and tenements in the said county of Cornwall, so that no sheriff or other bailiff or minister of Us or Our heirs enter those lands, or tenements, or fees to execute the said writs and summonses, or attachments, as well in pleas of the crown as in the others aforesaid, or do any other official act (*officium*) there, except in default of the said duke and other dukes of the said place, and his and their bailiffs or ministers in his and their lands, tenements, and fees aforesaid; And also that they have the chattels of their men and tenants in all the county aforesaid, being felons and fugitives, so that if any of their same men or tenants ought for his offence to lose life or limb, or shall flee and refuse to stand to justice (*judicio stare noluerit*), or shall commit any other offence for which be ought to lose his chattels, wheresoever justice ought to be done upon him, whether in the Court of Us or Our heirs or in any other Court, the said chattels shall belong to the said duke and the said other dukes aforesaid, and that it be lawful to them and their ministers, without hindrance of Us and of Our heirs and of others Our bailiffs or ministers whatsoever, to put themselves in seisin of the chattels aforesaid, and to retain them to the use of the said duke and of the other dukes; and also that they for ever have all fines for trespasses and other offences whatsoever, and also fines *pro licentia concordandi*, and all amerciaments, ransoms, issues forfeited, and forfeitures, year day and waste and strip, also the things which to Us and Our heirs may belong of such year day and waste, and of murders, from all the men and tenants of their said lands, tenements, and fees in the said county of Cornwall, in whatsoever Court of Us and of Our heirs it shall happen that these men and tenants are, which before us and Our heirs, and in the chancery of Us and Our heirs, and before the treasurer and barons of Us and Our heirs of the Exchequer, and before the justices of Us and Our heirs of the Bench, and before the steward and marshal and clerk of the market of the household (*hospitii*) of Us and Our heirs, for the time being, and in all other the Courts of Us and Our heirs, as also before justices itinerant for common pleas and pleas of the forest, and any other justices of Us and Our heirs, as well in the presence as in the absence of Us and Our heirs, make fines or be amerced, forfeit issues, or that forfeitures and murders shall be adjudged against them; which fines, amerciaments, ransoms, issues, day year and waste or strip, forfeitures and murders to Us and Our heirs would belong if they had not been granted to the said duke and the other dukes aforesaid; so that the same duke and other dukes aforesaid, by themselves or by their bailiffs or ministers, may levy, perceive, and have such fines, amerciaments, ransoms, issues and forfeitures of their men and tenants aforesaid, and all things which to Us and Our heirs might belong of the day year and waste or strip, and murders aforesaid, without question or hindrance from Us and Our heirs, justices, escheators, sheriffs coroners, and other bailiffs, or ministers whatsoever. Wherefore We will and firmly command for Us and Our heirs, that the said duke and the other dukes of the said place for the time being do for ever have the said liberties as is aforesaid, and do henceforward fully enjoy and use the same.

Witnesses, the venerable Fathers, John, Archbishop of Canterbury, Primate of all England, Our Chancellor; Henry, Bishop of Lincoln, Our treasurer; Roger, Bishop of Coventry and Lichfield; Thomas, Earl of Norfolk and Marshal of England; Our most dear uncles, Richard, Earl of Arundel, and Thomas, Earl of Warr; Thomas Wake, of Lydell; John de Mowbray; John Darcey, le Neveu, Steward of our Household, and others. Given by Our hand at Westminster, the XVIIlth day of March, in the eleventh year of Our reign.

By the King himself and all the council in Parliament

Charter
11 Edward III[272]

(3rd January 1338)

Edward, by the grace of God, King of England, Lord of Ireland, and Duke of Aquitaine, to his archbishops, bishops, abbots, priors, earls, barons, justices, sheriffs, reeves, ministers, and all his bailiffs and lieges, greeting. Know, that whereas We lately willing to honour the person of Our faithful and beloved Edward, Earl of Chester, Our first begotten son, did give to Our said son the name and honour of duke of Cornwall, and appointed him to be duke of Cornwall, and girded him with a sword, as it behoved, and that he the state and honour of a duke might be able to maintain in a manner becoming the nobility of his race, and support his charges attaching to such high honor, did give and grant by Our charter, for Us and Our heirs, to Our said son the shrievalty of Cornwall, with the appurtenances, also the castle, borough, manor and honor of Launceneton and divers other castles, boroughs, towns, manors, and honours, in the same county and elsewhere To have and to hold to the said duke and the eldest sons of him and his heirs kings of England, being dukes of the same place and heirs apparent to the said kingdom of England, together with the knights fees, advowsons of churches, and all other things to the said castles, boroughs, towns, manors, and honours in anywise belonging, from Us and Our heirs for ever, as in Our charter thereof to the said duke made is more fully contained, We, willing to provide more abundantly for Our

---

272 Manning, J., *Reports of cases argued and determined in the Court of Kings Bench during Michaelmas Term Ninth Geo IV* (1830) p 485-488

said son, have given and granted for Us and Our heir, and by this Our charter have confirmed to the said duke all Our fees, with the appurtenances which We have in the said county of Cornwall, or which do or shall (*poterunt*) belong or appertain to Us; To have and to hold to the said duke and the first begotten sons of him and of his heirs, king of England, being dukes of the said place and heirs apparent to the said kingdom of England as aforesaid, together with. wards, marriages, reliefs, escheats, forfeitures, and all other profits, issues, and emoluments which belong or shall belong to Us by reason of those fees, or which We and Our heirs might perceive and have if we had retained these fees in Our hands, from all and singular as well those who now hold the fees so by Us given and granted with the said county of Cornwall and those who shall hereafter hold the same, as also from the tenants holding of those fees, when they shall happen, notwithstanding Our prerogative in that behalf, and notwithstanding that the tenants who hold those fees or the tenants who hold of those fees may hold of Us or of Our heirs of Our crown or otherwise, in chief or in any other manner without the said county or within, of Us and Our heir, for ever. Which fees, with the appurtenances all other things aforesaid, as they are above specified, We for Us and Our heirs annex to the said duchy and unite so to remain for ever in the same manner as the said castle, boroughs, towns, manors, and honour. are annexed to the same, so that the same be in no wise severed from the said duchy at any time nor be given or in any wise granted by Us or Our heirs to any other person or persons than to the said dukes of the said place. And moreover We have granted of Our more abundant grace to the said Duke, for Us and Our heirs, that he and the first-begotten sons of him and his heir, kings of England, being dukes of the same place and heirs apparent to the said kingdom of England, do for ever have the returns of all writs of Us and Our heirs, and of summonses of the

Exchequer of Us and Our heirs, and attachments, as well in pleas of the Crown as in all others, as well in the same fees, as also in other fees which are held of the same in the said county of Cornwall; so that no sheriff, or other bailiff or minister of Us or Our heirs enter those fees to execute the said writs and summonses or to make attachments, as well in pleas of the Crown as in the others aforesaid, or do any other official act (*officium*) there, except in default of the said Duke and other Dukes of the said place, and his and their bailiff and minister aforesaid; and also that they have the chattels of the tenants holding the fees, and also of the tenants holding of their fees in the county aforesaid, being felons and fugitives, so that if any of the same tenants ought for his offence to lose life or limb, or shall flee and refuse to stand to justice (*Judicio stare noluerit*), or shall commit any other offence for which be ought to lose his chattels, wheresoever justice ought to be done upon him, whether in the Court of Us or Our heir, or in any other Court, the said chattels shall belong to the said Duke and the other Dukes aforesaid, and that it be lawful for them and their ministers, without hindrance of Us or of Our heirs or of other Our bailiffs or ministers whatsoever, to put themselves in seisin of the chattels aforesaid, and to retain them to the use of the said Duke and of the said other Dukes; and also that they for ever have all fines for trespasses and other offences whatsoever, and also fines pro *licentia concordandi*, and all amerciaments, ransoms, issues forfeited and forfeitures, year day, and waste and strip, and all things which to Us and Our heirs may belong of the said year day and waste and likewise of murders from all tenants holding their fees, and holding of their fees, in the said county, in whatsoever Court of Us and of Our heirs it shall happen that these tenants, as well before Us and Our heirs and in the Chancery of Us and our heirs and before the Treasurer and Barons of Us and Our heirs of the Exchequer, and before the Justices of Us and Our heirs of the Bench, and before the steward and marshal and clerk of the market of the household of Us and Our heirs for the time being, and in all other the Courts of Us and Our heirs, as also before justices itinerant for common pleas and pleas of the forest, and any other justices and ministers of Us and Our heirs, as well in the presence as in the absence of Us and Our heirs, make fines, or be amerced, forfeit issues, or that forfeitures and murder shall be adjudged against them, which fines, amerciaments, ransoms, issues, year day and waste or strip, forfeitures and murders, to Us and Our heirs would belong if they had not been granted to the said Duke and the other Dukes aforesaid, so that the same Duke and other Dukes aforesaid by themselves, or by their bailiffs and ministers may levy, perceive, and have such fines, amerciaments, issues, and forfeitures of such tenants, and all things which to Us and Our heirs might belong of the said year, day, and waste or strip and murders, without question or hindrance from Us and Our heirs, justices, escheators, sheriffs, coroners, and other bailiffs or ministers whatsoever: Also We have granted to the said Duke for Us and Our heirs, and by the charter have confirmed, that he and the first-begotten sons as aforesaid of him and his heirs, Kings of England, being Dukes of the same place and heirs apparent to the said kingdom of England, do have and hold all fees to the aforesaid castles, boroughs, towns, manors and honours, and other lands and tenements, whatsoever, which we gave to the said Duke by another charter, and caused to be annexed and united to the said duchy, in the said county of Cornwall, in any wise belonging, together with wards, marriages, reliefs, escheats, forfeitures, and other profits, issues, and emoluments whatsoever, which belong or shall belong to Us by reason of those fees in the same county, or which We or Our heirs might and ought to perceive and have if the said fees had been retained in the hands of Us and Our heirs, as well from all and singular the tenants who now hold or who hereafter shall hold the said fees as from the tenants holding of the said fees within the said county whenever the same shall happen, notwithstanding Our prerogative, or that the tenants holding the said fees, or the tenants holding of the said fees may hold elsewhere of Us and of Our heirs, or of the crown or otherwise in chief, or in any other manner, without the said county or within. We have granted also to the said Duke for us and our heirs, that be perceive and have scutage and profit of scutage as well of the fees aforesaid as also of all other fees belonging to the said castles, manors, honors, lands and tenements which We have lately granted to the said Duke as being annexed and united to the said dukedom, as well without as within the said county of Cornwall, and also of the knights fees belonging to the earldom of Chester within our said kingdom of England, viz. 40 shillings de scuto, or more or less, as it should happen, that We or Our heirs levied and bad de scuto as well of the first year of our reign, and of any other time since we took upon ourselves the government of Our kingdom as also in times future whilst be shall hold the said duchy, notwithstanding the said fees in the said first year or since have been in Our hands or in the hands of others, so as that We ought to have the scutage thereof, and notwithstanding that the said Duke may not hitherto have had or in future have his service in our wars, of Scotland or elsewhere by reason of which service he ought to receive such scutage. Wherefore we will and firmly command for Us and Our heirs, that the said Duke and other dukes of that place for the time being for ever have the fees aforesaid with the appurtenances and all other profits aforesaid, and also the liberties aforesaid and that they henceforth fully enjoy and use the said liberties and every of them, and that the said Duke as well in the said past time as henceforward as long as he shall hold the said duchy, do have and receive the scutage aforesaid and the profit thereof, is as aforesaid.

Witnesses, the venerable Fathers ,J. Archbishop of Canterbury, Primate of all England; R. Bishop of Coventry and Lichfield; R. Bishop of Chichester, Our Chancellor; Hugh de Courteney, Earl of Devon; Henry de Beaumont, Earl of Boghan, William de Clynton, Earl of Huntingdon; William de Ros de Hamelak, Henry de Ferrar, John Darcy, steward of Our household, and others.

Given by Our hand at the Tower of London, the third day of January, in the 11th year of Our reign.

The "Fordington" Charter
16 Edward III[273]

(9th July 1343)

For the Duke of Cornwall—The King to his Archbishops, Bishops, Abbots Priors Earls, Barons Justices, Sheriffs, Provosts, Ministers, and all Bailiffs and all his faithful subjects greeting. We consider it to be worthy and agreeable to reason that we who willingly show our hand profusely munificent to our beloved (subjects) also to foreigners, that we should grant with a certain abundance of more full munificence to our first born (Son), Edward Duke of Cornwall and Earl of Chester, who hath been born to us to the joy both of our subjects, the presage of lasting defence, and the strength and honor of our Royal House, considering, therefore, how the Earldom of Cornwall, now called the Duchy of Cornwall, hath sustained for a length of time a great dismemberment of its rights, and desiring to make integral (*redintegrare*) the said Duchy and re-collect its rights thus dispersed, in consideration of the premises we have given and granted for us and our heirs to the aforesaid Duke, the Manor of Little Weldon with its appurtenances, in the county of Northampton, the Manor of Fordington with the Hamlet of Whitewell, and other its appurtenances. in the County of Dorset, the Hamlet of Wyke Southteigne, with its appurtenances, in the County of Devon, and a certain tenement, with it appurtenances, in Shorman, in the county of Sussex, which were lately members and appurtenances of the

---

273 Tidal Estuaries, Foreshore and Under-Sea Minerals within and around the Coast of the County of Cornwall 1854-1856 Arbitration by Sir John Patteson Appendix L

said Earldom of Cornwall, now the Duchy of Cornwall, and which our beloved and faithful Hugh de Ardele, Earl of Gloucester, and Margaret his wife, now deceased, held for the life of the same Margaret, by the grant of Edward, lately King of England, our father, and which by the death of the same Margaret are now in our hand. We have given also and granted for us and our heirs to the aforesaid Duke The Town (William) de Rokynham with its appurtenances, in the County of Northampton, which is a member, and among the appurtenances of the said Duchy, and which came to our hands by the death of John of Eltham, lately Earl of Cornwall, our most dear brother, who held the town aforesaid by our grant to have and to hold to the said Duke and his heirs, first born Sons of the Kings of England, hereditarily to succeed to the Kingdom of England, of us and our heirs for ever by the services therefore due and accustomed, as annexed and united to the said Duchy, together with the Knights' fees, advowsons of churches, and all other things to the aforesaid manors, towns, hamlets, tenements in anywise relating, in the same manner in which the aforesaid Duchy was granted to him by us. Wherefore we will and firmly command for us and our heirs, that the aforesaid Duke should have and hold the manors, towns, hamlets and tenements aforesaid, to the aforesaid Duke and his said heirs for ever as annexed and united to the aforesaid Duchy, together with the fees, advowsons, and ether their appurtenances aforesaid of us and our heirs as is aforesaid. These persons being witnesses, &c., &c.

Given under our hand at the 'Tower of London", the 9th day of July.

By Writ of Privy Seal.

INSPEXIMUS CHARTER
of
KING HENRY VII[274]

(30th April 1488)

Henry by the grace of God King of England and France and Lord of Ireland, to all to whom the present letters shall come, Greeting. We have inspected the confirmatory Letters Patent of the Lord Edward IV, late King of England, in these words:

[Here follows a recital of the Inspeximus charter of King Edward IV, reciting that of King Richard II, reciting that of King Edward III, reciting those of King John and Earl Richard;]

Now we, considering the aforesaid charters and letters, and all and singular in them contained to be valid and agreeable, do accept and approve them for us and our heirs, as far as in us lies, and do now ratify and confirm them to our beloved burgesses of the said borough and their heirs and successors as the aforesaid letters reasonably bear witness and as the same burgesses and their ancestors have always hitherto reasonably used and enjoyed the said liberties and exemptions. In witness whereof we have caused these our letters to be made patent. Witness myself at Westminster the thirtieth day of April in the third year of our reign. shillings paid in Chancery. Examined by us, Richard Skypton and William Elyot, clerks. Bagot.

---

274 Tidal Estuaries, Foreshore and Under-Sea Minerals within and around the Coast of the County of Cornwall 1854-1856 Arbitration by Sir John Patteson Appendix L

Appendix V

Scilly Islands
Cornwall

1833

Copy Opinion of the Law Officers of the Crown[275]

It is to be regretted that in a matter of so much importance here should not be a regular series of Authentic public documents by referring to which the question between the Crown and the Duchy of Cornwall might be at once satisfactorily decided.

This however (owing to accident or neglect in past times) is not the case and the conclusion now to be arrived at, is one derived rather from argument and inference, than from positive and direct evidence.

We have carefully examined the copies of the several documents submitted to us together with the very able statements and arguments and elaborate researches which accompany them And we are of the opinion upon the whole that the Scilly Islands are to be considered as part of the possessions of the Duchy of Cornwall and that they do not belong to the Crown *jura Coronae*.[276]

And we are further of opinion under all the circumstances of the case that there is not any sufficient ground for our advising the Crown to call in question the right of the Duchy as it has been asserted and enjoyed for the last 40 years.

> Wm. Horne
> J Campbell
> Lincolns Inn January 1833

275 TNA BT 297/556 – St Mary's Pier, Scilly Isles: Mr Dorrien Smith and Duchy of Cornwall (1889 - 1922)
276 The Crown Royal Rights and Prerogatives

Appendix VI

Law Officers Opinion Regarding Royal Mines 1860

Mining Rights; claim by Duchy of Cornwall[277]

OPINION

We have considered the statements laid before us as to the claim of H.R.H. the Duke of Cornwall to the gold and silver mines within the County of Cornwall and we have had the advantage of a personal conference with the Attorney General of the Duchy on the subject.

We are not satisfied that the facts and matters relied on in support of the claim are in anywise sufficient to countervail the general principle of law that Royal Mines are a Prerogative Right of so high a character as not to pass by any royal grant except by express words of which we find none in the Charters by which the Duchy of Cornwall was created and its possessions granted.

It is however not seemly or proper that a question of this kind between Her Majesty and the Prince should be the subject of legal proceedings and in the course of our conference with the Prince's Attorney General it appeared to us and which view as we understood met with his full concurrence that the question should be considered by some former Judge of the Highest position and eminence. And it was suggested that possible Lord Cranworth might be induced to accept the reference.

The Settlement of this question need not delay the proceedings against the persons taking the Royal Mines—Application should be made in the joint names of the Crown

277   TNA TS 27/818 Treasure Trove—Gold ornaments found at Amalevor Farm (1907—1932)

Officers and the Duchy Officers and if persons working should be willing to accept of proper licenses that royalties payable could be paid to a joint account to be held until settlement of the question is proposed.

If it is necessary to take proceedings they might also be taken pending settlement of the question but such proceedings will be more properly taken in the name of the Queen it being clearly understood beforehand that such course was adopted for convenience only and really on behalf of both and without in any way prejudicing the case of the Prince.

Richard Bethell
W M Jones Wm Atherton
Lincolns Inn 29 May 1860

Appendix VII

Articles of Agreement Between Crown And Duchy of Cornwall 1620

ARTICLES[278] of agreement conceyved and propounded the twelvethe day of June in the years of the raigne of our Soveraigne Lord James by the grace of God of England, Scotland, / Fraunce and Ireland Kinge Defendor of the faith etc. viz. of England Fraunce and Ireland the Seaventeenth and of Scotland the two and fiftyeth BETWEENE Sir Lyonell Cranfeild knight Master./ of the Kinges Maties Wardes and Liveryes Sr Benjamin Ruddierd Knight Survayor of his Maties Liveryes Sr Jame Ley Knight Attorney of his Maties Courte of Wardes and Liveryes Sr / Myles Fleetwood Knight Receavor generall of the same Courte for and on the behalf of his Matie there vnto authorised by the kings Maties Lres vnder his Signett of the one parte And Sr / Henry Hobart Knight and Baronett Lord Cheife Justice of his Maties Courte of Comon pleas at Westminster and Chauncellor of the most excellent Prince Charles Prince of Wales Duke of / Cornwall and of

Yorke and Earle of Chester Sr James Fullerton knight Mt of his Highnes Wardes Sr Charles Chibbourne knight his Highnes Serieant at lawe Sr John Walter knight his / Highnes Attorney generall and Sr Thomas Trevor knight his Hignes Sollicitor generall for and on the behalf of the said Prince his Highnes thervnto authorised by commande from / his Highnes of the other parte as followeth vizt.

   Whereas many differences and questions must needs arise from tyme to tyme touching the enjoying of the bodyes and landes of Wardes whose Auncestors did hold lande of the kinge Matie in Capite or otherwise by knighte/ service And alsoe held other landes of the Prince his Highnes in Capite or by Common knights service as of his dutchie of Cornewall or Earledome of Chester or otherwise by reason of the intermeddling of theire severall tenures and the tytles / between his Matie and his Highnes which is most convenyent and necessary it us vpon mature deliberation had by the said persons authorised as aforesaid proposed That it shall soe please his most excellent Matie and the Prince his /Highnes the course hereafter following in certayne Articles expressed by by his Maties Privy Seale of warrant to the Master and Councell of his Courte of Wardes and Lyveries on his Mats parte there decreed And by like warrant of his Highnes / accepted ratified and approved.

FIRST whereas most of the lande within the County of Cornewall are held of his Hignes as duchie of Cornewall and otherwise And most of the landes in the Countys of Chester and Flint are held of his Hignes as Earle of Chester and/ otherwise And also dyvers honors Mannors and landes lying inother forrayne Countyes are parcel of the duchie of Cornewall and thereby dyvers lands lying out of the said County of Cornewall are held in like manner of the said Prince/ as of his duchie of Cornewall And whereas dyvers landes in the said severall Countyes of Cornewall Chester and Flynt are likewise held of his Matie in Capite or otherwise wth breedith greate vuncertainty and trouble in fyndeing out the/ tenures and offices therevpon and seising the bodyes and landes of such wards in the Countys aforesaid IT is therefore thought meete that his Matie would be pleased to permit that his Highnes may have the whole benefit of all his Mats tenures in the said Countyes of Cornewall Chester and Flynt for such profit and comodetie are arise within the said Countyes onely Aswell by graunde Serieantie knightes service in cheife as other tenures of all sortes And the bodyes and landes of all Wardes that shall growe by such tenures or Wardeshipps with the inincidentes and profits depending therevpon within the said Countyes soe farr as the same are or maybe within the government or jurisdiccion/ of his Maties Courte of Wards and Liveries IN consideracion whereof it is likewise thought meete that the kinges Matie shall have the benefit of all Wardeshippes mariages liveries and primer seisens of all such tenures in Capite knightes service or socage in cheife as shall belonge to his Hignes as Duke of Cornewall for lands lyinge in any place out of the County of Cornewall.

2. SECONDLY if any person doe or shall hold landes lying the Countyes of Cornwall Chester or Flint of the Kinges Majestie in Capite or by knightes service or of the Prince his Highnes in Capite or by knightes service and doe or shall also holde other landes of the kinge in Capite or by knightes service lying out of the said Countyes and doe dye his heire within age. In such case his Majestie shall have the wardeshipp of the bodye and mariage / onely of such heire being Warde BUT if in the case aforesaid any person doe or shall hold landes lying in the Countyes of Cornewall Chester or Flynt in Capite or knightes service of the kinges

Majesty or of the Princes Highnes / And also do or shall hold landes lying out of the Countie of Cornewall onely of the Prince in Capite or by knightes service as Duke of Cornewall, and dye his heirs within age. In such case the Prince shall have the / Wardshipp of the bodye and mariage of such heire being Warde.

3. THIRDLY if any person doe or shall holde landes in the Countyes of Cornewall Chester or Flynt of the kinges Majesty by knightes service in Capite and doe or shall likewise holde other landes within the said Countyes of Cornewall / Chester or Flynt or out of the said Countyes either of the Kinge or Prince or of other persons and dye his heirs within age In such case as concerning the Custodye and Wardshipp of the landes of such heire The Prince his/ Highnes shall have all the landes of such Wards lying or out of the said countyes if the said landes do hold of the dutchie of Cornwall in the Countyes of Cornewall Chester and Flynte And the kinges Majestie shall have all the landes of such wars lying out of the Countyes aforesaid not held of the said Dutchie And the like benefit/ to be taken where livery primier seisin or ouster le maine shalbe dewe upon any tenure whatsoever./

4. FOWERTHLY if any person doe or shall holde landes lying out of the said three Countyes of the kinge by knightes service in capite and doth or shall alsoe hold other lands lying within the Countyes of Cornewall Chester or Flynt/ and dye his heire within age whereby the kings Majestie by his prerogative is to have the Custody and profit of all the said landes with the said person helde the Prince his Hignes Notwithstanding shall have the custody and/ Profit of the said landes lying within the said countyes of Cornewall Chester or Flynt of whomsoever and in what manner soever the same be holden. And in like sorte if any be warde to his Majestie for landes lyinge out of the/ Countyes

aforesaid and afterwards during his minoritie lands lying within the said Countyes of Cornewall Chester or Flynt shall discende to the said Warde the Prince shall have the Custodye and benefit of the same lands./ The like Course to be holden liverie Premier seisin or Ouster le maine shalbe due vpon any tenure whatsoever…/

5. FIFTHLY it is thought meete that the Prince his Hignes his assignees and Committees shall have the ayde and assistance of his Majesties Courte of Wards and Liveryes and may there in his Majesties name or in his or theire owne as the Case shall require for all the Proffittes and benefittes of all sortes belonging to his Highnes by the true intent and meaning of theis presents. /

6. LASTLY it is thought meete and Conveyent that if any question shall here after arise between the Master of the Courte of Wards and other of the Consell of the said Court for the tyme being and the Chauncellor to his Hignes and other the Commissioners of His Hignes likewise for the tyme being concerning/ tenures or any incidents or dependancies therevpon then the same shall first be debated and discussed between the said Officers respectively (and if it may be) determined without suite in lawe.

Appendix VIII

Board of Inland Revenue
Instructions

and

Law Officers Opinion

1913

The Duchy of Cornwall[279]

Draft
OPINION
for A.G.

15th August 1913

SOLICITOR OF INLAND REVENUE

L.O.D. 18TH AUGUST 13

---

279 TNA L/O 3/467—Law Officers Opinion 1913

THE DUCHY OF CORNWALL OPINION

WE ARE OF OPINION THAT the same principles which render the provisions of an Act of Parliament inapplicable to the Crown unless the Crown is expressly named, apply also to the Prince of Wales in his capacity as Duke of Cornwall. This results from the peculiar title of the Prince of Wales to the Duchy of Cornwall. In other respects the Prince of Wales as being the first subject of the Crown, is, like other subjects, bound by Statutory enactments.

Taxation is not and cannot be exacted from land; it is exacted from subjects who are tax payers. For the reason given in our answer to the first question, the Duke of Cornwall is not liable to such taxation, but it may be that he will not wish to insist upon his privilege of exemption. In view of the fact that the property in the hands of the Duchy of Cornwall may change from time to time, it is in a high degree inconvenient that valuations should not proceed in the ordinary course in respect of land now belong to the Duchy, and we think that the Duchy of Cornwall should be strongly urged (without raising any question of legal rights on one side or the other) to make returns and co-operate in getting valuations settled.

We would strongly deprecate the bringing to an issue of questions such as those here set out. It is obvious that if such a matter were litigated the Duchy of Cornwall might find that even though they succeeded their success in the Courts did not conclude the matter. The practice which as we are instructed, is followed by the Crown itself, is one which avoids raising these awkward and difficult questions and we are of opinion that representation should be made to the advisers of the Duchy as to the propriety, while expressly saving what they conceive to be their legal rights of exemption, of making concessions as of grace.

RE THE DUCHY OF CORNWALL

Copy

INSTRUCTIONS

— to —

the Law Officers and Mr Finlay to advise

Solicitor of Inland Revenue

RE
THE DUCHY OF CORNWALL

INSTRUCTIONS
To the Law Officers and Mr. Finlay to advise

The opinion of the Law Officers and Mr Finlay is desired with reference to a questions which has arisen between the Board of the Inland Revenue and the Duchy of Cornwall, namely, whether the Officers of the Duchy are bound to make returns for the purpose of Mineral Rights Duty in accordance with the provisions of Section 20(3) of the Finance (1909-10) Act 1910.

A copy of the correspondence which has passed between the Secretary to the Duchy and the Board of the Inland Revenue is transmitted herewith, and it will be seen that the duty to give particulars under Section 20 of the Finance Act is resisted by the Duchy upon the broad ground that the Prince of Wales possesses the same prerogatives as the King, and that inasmuch as the King is not bound by the provisions of a statute unless expressly named, the Prince of Wales either absolutely or at all events so far as the lands of the Duchy of Cornwall are concerned, is not bound by the provisions of the Finance Act 1910.

A conference between the Secretary to the Duchy and the Solicitor of Inland Revenue has led to no practical result, as neither was able to admit the contentions of the other, and accordingly the Board of Inland Revenue desire to be advised as to the correctness in law of the contention of the Duchy, and as to the course to be adopted in view of it.

The general proposition that the Crown is not bound unless expressly named in a statute is of course beyond dispute, and has been affirmed by many authorities and cases of which the following are all that need here be referred to:—

Chitty Prerogative of the Crown 383
R v Cook 3 T.R. 519[280]
Weymouth v Nugent 6 B & S 22[281]
Mersey Docks v Cameron 11 H.L.C. 443[282]
Ex parte Postmaster General L.R. 10 C.D. 595[283]
Re Oriental Bank L.R. 28 C.D. 643[284]

But that the Prince of Wales who is a subject, though the first of His Majesty's subjects, possesses the same privilege is a proposition which it is submitted cannot be inferred from mere general words such as a statement that the "Lord Prince shall have therewith (i.e. with the Duchy of Cornwall) the King's Prerogative" (see Mr. Peacocks letter of 20 February 1911) because this particular prerogative of the Crown is one which is quite distinct, and differs not merely in degree but in substance from other prerogative rights of the Crown such as escheats, foreshore, royal fish, etc which can be and have been granted by the King to a subject. The King has not power to dispense with laws or the execution of laws (see Bill of Rights 1 Will & Mary Session 2 c.2) and he could not by exercise of the prerogative prevent the application to the Prince of Wales of the provisions of an Act of Parliament, and if the grant of the Duchy to the Prince affected to carry any such right or privileges it is submitted that any such grant would be inoperative.

---

280 *R v Cook* (1790) (3 T.R. 519)
281 *Weymouth v Nugent* (1865) (6 B & S 22)
282 *Mersey Docks v Cameron* (1865) (11 H.L.C. 443)
283 *Ex parte Postmaster General* (1879) (L.R. 10 C.D. 595)
284 *Re Oriental Bank* (1884) (LR. 28 C.D. 643)

AN INTRODUCTION TO THE LAWS OF CORNWALL, SCILLY, AND DEVON

Further, the passage in Staunford to which Mr Peacock refers is apparently to be found on p 11 under title "Wardes". The words are as follows:

> "Like law is it, if the King grant an honour to the Lord Prince and his heires Kings of England, it seemth by the better opinion in M.21 Ed. 3 folio 41 that the Lord Prince shall have the therewith the King's Prerogative, because it is not severed from the Crowne after the forme as it is given, for the none shall have inheritance therof but Kings of this Realme"

The prerogative right here dealt with is that of wardship, and the passage would appear to be no authority for the possession of the Prince of Wales of all prerogative rights whatever including the special privilege now in dispute.

Search has been made for any authority directly laying down the proposition that the Duke of Cornwall qua his rights over Duchy lands, or that the Prince of Wales, as such, is not bound by statute unless expressly named. No such authority has been found and Mr Peacock when pressed on the point was not able to point to any such authority.

The question appears, however, to have been raised in the case of *Attorney General to the Prince of Wales v Crossman* (L.R. 1 Ex 381).[285] In that case the Defendant to an information filed by the Attorney General to the Prince of Wales applied to change the venue. In the course of the argument the Attorney General of the Duchy raised the point that the Crown was not bound by the statutes and practice as to change of venue and that the Prince of Wales sueing in right of the royal possession of the Duchy enjoyed the same right (see p 383)

The Court however did not decide this point, holding that the balance of convenience was in favour of trying the case in

---

285 *Attorney General to the Prince of Wales v Crossman* (1866) (L.R. 1 Ex 381)

London as desired by the Prince. The decision was therefore in favour of the Duchy on other grounds.

In support of the existence of the special prerogative right claimed in respect of the Duchy lands the Secretary to the Duchy puts forward several arguments which appear to be the following effect:

(1) That the prerogative rights of the Duchy are identical with those of the Crown

(2) That express mention is made of the Duchy in Acts of Parliament when those Acts are intended to apply to the Duchy, the inference being that Acts of Parliament would not so apply without express mention.

(3) That it has been the practice to treat Duchy lands in Government Bills in precisely the same way as Crown lands the inference being that the position and prerogative rights are the same in both cases.

(4) That in fact Duchy lands are Crown lands and the same principles apply to both

For these propositions various authorities are cited which counsel will consider, but in respect of which the following considerations are submitted.

(1) As to the identity of the prerogative rights of the Duchy and Crown.

The passage cited from Staunford has been dealt with above. It does not deal with the specific prerogative right here claimed. Undoubtedly many prerogative rights of the Crown are possessed by the Duchy but the right here in question is, it is submitted, a special right which the Crown has not power to grant at all still less to confer by general grant.

The passage cited from the judgment in *Attorney General for the Prince of Wales v St Aubyn* (Wightwicks Reports at p.240 per Graham B)[286] must be read in connection with the context. The judgment is there dealing with the peculiar features of the charter granting the Duchy in connection with the question whether the Prince could sue by his Attorney General. No question of any other right was under consideration. It seems clear that the only right of the Crown there dealt with by the judgment was the right to sue by a special officer and in special form. The question was one of legal procedure only. The wide application claimed for the passage cited cannot, it is submitted, be maintained.

With regard to the practice of obtaining the assent of the Prince of Wales, as well as of the Sovereign to the introduction of bills in Parliament affecting the Duchy or Crown lands (see May's Parliamentary Practice, Tenth Edition p 423) it is suggested this usage is merely a usage of Parliament and does not affect the legal question. For what is worth, however, the usage certainly shows that it is the custom to treat Crown lands and Duchy lands in this particular respect on the same footing. It is understood however that the Treasury Solicitor is unaware that the possessions of the Duchy, have, under instructions from the Treasury been always treated in Government bills in precisely the same way as Crown lands, and that the Parliamentary Counsel are also unaware of any such instructions. It is considered by the Treasury Solicitor that it would not be correct to make such general statement with regard to Duchy lands, and that the position might, and probably would, vary according to circumstances.

(2) With reference to the point that express mention is made of the Duchy in Acts of Parliament intended to bind the

---

286 *Attorney General to H.R.H. Prince of Wales, Duke of Cornwall v Sir John St. Aubyn and others* (1811) Wight 167)

Duke of Cornwall, it must be conceded that it has been the practice to deal expressly with the Duchy and Duchy lands in Acts of Parliament, and other instances might be cited in addition to those given by Mr Peacock (e.g. section 23 of the Arbitration Act 1889 52, 53Victoria c.49) But it would appear to be going too far to say that in default of express statutory provisions the statutes of limitation would not apply to the Duke of Cornwall. In the case of *Attorney General for Prince of Wales v St Aubyn* at p 238 of Wightwick's report Graham B. states expressly that these statutes apply to the Prince when exercising the prerogative of the Crown to sue by his Attorney General by information of intrusion in the same way as they apply to the Crown when exercising that prerogative right. The specific statutes to which he referred were the Act 21 Jac. 1. cap 14[287] in which the Duke of Cornwall and the Duchy lands were not mentioned and the *nullum tempus* Act of 1769 (9 Geo IIIc. 16).[288] It is therefore not clear that the enactment of express provisions as to limitations of actions in the case of the Duchy of Cornwall (as to which see 7 & 8 Vict. C. 105 Sections 13, 14, 71, 73[289] and 23, 24 Vict. c.53)[290] were necessitated by the fact that the Duke of Cornwall was not bound by statutes of limitation which bound the Crown or the subject or indeed by any statute unless expressly named therein, and if the judgment of Graham B. is correct it would appear that in this instance the Duke was stated to be bound though not expressly or by necessary intendment referred to. See further on this point *Attorney General v Mayor of Plymouth* Wightwick at pp 148, 159, 164.[291]

---

287 Intrusions Act 1623
288 Crown Suits Act 1769 (*nullum tempus act*)
289 Duchy of Cornwall Act 1844
290 Duchy of Cornwall (limitation of actions etc) Act 1860
291 *Attorney General to H.R.H. Prince of Wales, Duke of Cornwall v Mayor and Commonalty*

(3) It is no doubt the case that Duchy lands are dealt with in Acts of Parliament in a similar way to Crown lands. So are lands of the Duchy of Lancaster which are Crown lands. The Duchy is entitled to press the argument from this fact to the fullest extent, but it is submitted that even when so pressed that argument does not go very far.

(4) The most important point made on behalf of the Duchy would seem to be last, namely, that the Duchy lands are in effect part of the lands of the Crown and that any prerogative of the Crown which would be available to the Crown must be equally available with regard to those lands when in the hands of the Duke of Cornwall, and that therefore, if lands of the Crown would not be affected by a revenue law imposing a tax on lands, lands of the Duchy would equally be unaffected. It is submitted however that even if this be the case Mineral Rights Duty is not a tax on lands at all, it is a tax on the rental value of rights to work minerals and of mineral way leaves. It is a tax on profits of a certain class and not imposed on land as land.

The general nature of the rights and position of the Duke of Cornwall are to be found set out in the *Prince's Case* (8 Rep p.1).[292] That case appears to have decided that the charter granting the Duchy of Cornwall was granted by authority of Parliament and is sufficient in itself without needing any other Act to support it, that the Prince had a fee simple in the Duchy, and that judicial notice is to be taken of the Charter. Other cases in point are *Attorney General v St Aubyn* (Wightwicks Reports p 167) and *Rowe v Brenton* (Reported by Concanen, and also to be found in 8 B & C 737 and 3 M. & Ry. 133).[293] As regards

to the Borough of Plymouth (1754) (Wight 134)

292 *The Princes Case* (1606) (8 Rep 1a) (77 E.R. 481)

293 *Rowe v Brenton* (1828) (8 B & C 737) (3 Man & Ry K.B. 133) (108 E.R. 1217)

the lands of the Duchy in Wightwick p.242 it is stated that the King may protect the Duchy lands by his privilege of information by the Attorney General and that "the privilege exists for the protection of the Crown lands; the Duchy lands "are part of them as a member of the Royal Establishment; The Crown has at all times an interest in them "there is the same expediency and use of the prerogative to "protect them, when the Prince has them as when the King…"

Similarly in *Rowe v Brenton* (3 Man & Ry. at p.158) on the question of the admissibility in evidence of a document on the ground it was a public document, it being produced from Duchy records, Lord Tenterden said "The objection is put upon the grounds that this is a private document, and that the Duke of Cornwall is to be considered merely as any other of His Majesty's subjects, excepting only his very high rank. But I am clearly of opinion that the Duke of Cornwall is not to be considered as a private subject; when there is no Duke of Cornwall, the Duchy belongs to the Crown; it is sometimes in the hands of the Duke, sometimes in the hands of the Crown. The Crown therefore, or in other words the public, has an interest in everything that is done in the Duchy; and it appears to me perfectly immaterial whether the act done is done under the authority of the King or under the authority of the Duke, when there is a Duke and in all these matters the interest of the Crown is equally concerned."

Again at p224 (c.f. also argument of Dampier on p 221) Lord Tenterden says "considering the very peculiar nature of the Duchy of Cornwall, whether the Duchy be vested in the Crown or in the Duke, the Crown has a peculiar interest in it at all times, and whatever is done at any period is to be received in the same manner. I am of the opinion that whatever is done during the existence of a Duke, is to be treated in the same manner as if it were done by the Crown".

(Concanen's Rep 1)

It was thereupon decided (see p. 226 per Littledale J.) that the same rules by which leases from which the Crown are authenticated prevailed in the case of leases granted by the Duke of Cornwall. It must be admitted therefore that as regards the lands which form part of the Duchy the Crown retains some special and peculiar interest, and that Duchy lands while in the hands of the Prince are not precisely in the same position as lands in the hands of a subject. The question is whether this peculiar interest is sufficient to carry with it as attached to the lands the special prerogative of the Crown which ensures that lands of the Crown shall not, without express provision, be affected by Acts of Parliament. It has been submitted above, first that the tax sought to be imposed in this case is not a tax on lands at all, and secondly that eve if it be so regarded, then that this peculiar prerogative is different in substance from other prerogative rights. If this be so the arbitration proceedings of 1858 (a copy of which is sent herewith) which are called in aid by the Duchy are to a great extent irrelevant. In the proceedings in 1855—1858 the point in issue seem to have been (1) whether Duchy rights extended to the sea bed within the three mile limit (2) whether the soil of the ports of the Duchy of Cornwall was parcel of the Duchy and (3) whether at the least such portions of the sea bed should be held to be within the County as might be considered to be within the jurisdiction, under Common Law, of County Officers, or of the inquest and Court held for a County. The claims of the Duchy was supported by showing, inter alia the exercise by Officers of the Duchy of such prerogative rights as the Crown enjoys over Crown lands, in the area in question.

In 1904 the precise question which now arises was raised in consequence of a dispute between the Admiralty and the Duchy with regard to the fundus and foreshore of Plymouth Harbour. A copy of the case submitted to the Law Officers is attached and Counsel is referred to the arguments and

190

authorities there put forward. No opinion was written on this reference but it is understood that the Attorney General (Sir R Finlay) conferred with the Attorney General to the Duchy (Sir A Cripps) and that a settlement was arrived at which rendered it unnecessary for the legal opinion to be determined. The Admiralty have been requested to furnish any information at their disposal with reference to the nature of the settlement arrived at and with copies of any documents and authorities which may be of assistance and as soon as received there will be laid before Counsel.

It is understood that the Prince of Wales pays Income Tax but the Secretary to the Duchy states that a "bounty" is given by the Duchy in lieu of rates, similar, it is understood, to that which is contributed by the public revenue in respect of Government Buildings. It is assumed that the objection of the Duchy to paying rates is based on the same claim to prerogative rights as is raised in this case.

It may be mentioned that the Crown Private Estates Acts[294] do not appear to apply to the lands of the Duchy of Cornwall those lands being either expressly exempted, or excluded under the general provisions which prevent those Acts from applying to lands which are possessed by the Sovereign through inheritance from his predecessors. Otherwise the subjection of lands dealt with by those Acts to ordinary taxation might be held to apply to Duchy of Cornwall lands at all events while those lands are in the hands of the Crown.

Assuming that the Prince of Wales as Duke of Cornwall is bound by the Finance (1909-10) Act 1910 to pay Mineral Rights Duty, a further question arises as to whether during the minority of the Duke, which apparently continues for this purpose as long as he is under age 21 years any duty can be recovered or indeed is payable. During the minority of the

---

294   Crown Private Estates Act 1862 and 1873

Duke (See 5 Vict. Sess.2 cap 2[295] repealed by Section 1 of 26 27 Vict.c.49.[296] and Section 11 and 25, 26 Vict. c.49[297] and Section 38 of repealing Act, and compare 52 Geo IIIc.123, Section 11[298] and 25, 26 Vict. c.49)[299] the rights of management exercised by him are exercisable by the Sovereign or by persons acting under His authority and although all such rights are to be taken as having been done by the Duke and although the Duke himself may be bound by the Act though not expressly named, it may be argued that, having regard to the interest which the Sovereign has at all times in the Duchy and its lands, and the fact the He is exercising the rights of management by Himself as guardian or by His Officers, the prerogative of the Crown whatever may be the case when the Duke is of age, applies to the Duchy lands and, the Crown not being named in the Finance Act 1910 Mineral Rights Duty is not payable. It would appear therefore, that even if the Board of Inland Revenue be right upon the main question of principle raised in this case, the practical result may still be that no returns can be enforced and no duty can be recovered until after the Duke of Cornwall attains majority.

The Acts of Parliament relating to the Duchy of Cornwall will be found enumerated at p 1514 Volume 1 of the Chronological Table and Index of Statutes (Edition 1911) but an examination of these Acts has not thrown any further light upon the question now raised.

The following papers are transmitted herewith:-

295 Duchy of Cornwall Leases etc Act 1842
296 Duchy of Cornwall Management Act 1863
297 Duchy of Cornwall Lands Act 1862
298 Duchy of Cornwall Act 1812
299 Duchy of Cornwall Lands Act 1862

Correspondence between the Board of Inland Revenue and the Secretary to the Duchy.

Statements on behalf of the Crown and the Duchy of Cornwall upon reference to arbitration arising under the Cornwall Submarine Mines Act 1858 (One copy only is procurable)

Case prepared for the opinion of the Law Officers, Mr. Acland K.C., and Mr. Wills as to Crown and Duchy rights in Plymouth Harbour.

Copy Duchy saving clause as usually inserted in Acts of Parliament

The Law Officers and Mr Finlay are requested to advise:-

(1) Whether the contention of the Duchy of Cornwall that the Prince of Wales is not bound by Act of Parliament unless expressly named is correct.

(2) Whether it is the case that lands of the Duchy of Cornwall are not affected by the provisions of Acts imposing taxation unless express reference to or mention of those lands is made in such Act.

(3) Whether the Prince of Wales is bound to make returns and to pay Mineral Rights Duty in respect of the rental value of rights granted by the Duchy of Cornwall to work minerals and of mineral way leaves and if so how those returns can be enforced and the duty recovered.

(4) Whether during the minority of the Prince of Wales returns can be enforced and Mineral Rights Duty can be recovered in respect of rights to work minerals and mineral way leaves granted by the Duchy.

(5) What course should be pursued by the Commissioners in order to compel the rendering of returns and the payment of sums due in respect of Minerals Rights Duty which in

the opinion of Counsel the Prince of the Duchy are bound to pay.

(6) Generally

(The following are all in manuscript)

Re the Duchy of Cornwall

The principal question in this case is the position of the Duchy in respect to mineral rights Duty
Origin of the case

14 July 1910	*Notice sent to Duchy o make returns for the purpose of the mineral rights duty*
25 July 1910	*Duchy sent replies that as Part I of the Finance (1909-1910) Act 1910 does not apply to the Crown or the Duchy there is no necessity to make returns.*
	After some correspondence
20 Feb 1911	*Duchy write setting out their authorities for this proposition*
	(1) Passage in Staunford on Prerogative
	(2) Passage in Graham B's judgement in Pr of Wales v St Aubyn Wightwick at p 240
	(3) Acts intended to apply to Duchy have always been made expressly applicable. Certain acts are cited to show this, and reference is made to a statement in 1909 by the President of the Bd of Agr. In the Lords (Par. Deb' Lords 1909 vol 3 p 1058)
13 June	*Inland Revenue write that they are not satisfied.*
14 June	*Duchy write pointing out that Duchy land have always been treated in Govt bills like Crown lands refer to certain Acts of Parliament in support of this. Duchy also refer to*
	(1) Appendices prepared on behalf of the Duchy on the occasions of a dispute with the Crown in 1855-58 re Cornwall Foreshores.

(2) *The Princes Case 8 Co. Rep 1*

(3) *Concanen's report of Rowe v Brenton 1830*

14 July 1911   *Inland Rev. write that they are still not satisfied*

Position of the Duchy of Cornwall

Authorities

Princes Case

Chitty on Prerogative 1820 Edn pp 403-404

Comyns Digest Vol 7 p 203

The eldest son of the King becomes Duke of Cornwall without any creation and also becomes seised in fee simple of the lands of the Duchy of Cornwall without grant. In order to take without grant the eldest son must be the first born.

Till a prince is born the King is seised, but when born the prince is immediately seised in fee and leases made by the King may be determined by the prince.

It depends upon the terms of the original grant of 11 Ed 3 which has taken to be a charter confirmed by Parliament (see The Princes Case)

Reference may also be made to

1754 A.G. v Mayor of Plymouth—Wightwick 134 which decides (inter alia) (see p 149) that the statute of Limitations (as to the right of entry into lands) does not apply to the Duchy lands but ??? not ??? ground of prerogative, but on the ground of the form of the grant "The estate is indissoluble and inseparable".

At p 160 per Legge B

"As to his being in possession of it as a royal prerogative I do not know that the Prince of Wales in any instance differs from other subjects; though he is the greatest subject he is still only a subject; but his estate and possessions are as effectually secured here as if he had a personal prerogative; it is a Parliamentary prerogative, they have annexed it as a prerogative"

This passage down to "still only a subject" is cited by Wood B apparently with approval in his dissentient judgement in A G for Pr. Of Wales v St Aubyn Wightwick 167

At p 240 of this latter case occurs a passage relied on by the Duchy

(AG for Pr of Wales v St Aubyn at p 240)

Per Graham B

"for it forms part of my argument that the Prince of Wales stands as to these possessions precisely in the same situation that the King himself does, and that they are as entire and as much protected when they are in the possession of the Prince as when they are in the possession of the Crown and that for necessary purpose of preserving their integrity"

(Graham B is here dealing with the question whether the Prince could be disseised)

The decision in the case was that the Prince had a right to file an English information by his A.G. per land parcel of the Duchy of Cornwall

1828 Rowe v Brenton (Concanen's report 1830) (8 B & C 737)

This case decides (inter alia) that an account of the interest which the Crown has in the Duchy of Cornwall are to be considered as public acts.

At pp 756-7 of the B & C report it is held that for the purpose of certain evidence the king and the Duke of Cornwall must be considered as identified.

At p 756 it is stated in argument "It was decided very soon after the creation of the duchy that the Duke of Cornwall has possession of the Duchy with the same privilege as the king because it is never disannexed from the Crown"

The authority cited for this is statement in Fitzherberts Abr Prerog Ed 16

Which consists in a paraphrase and abridgement of a case report in the year Book 21 Ed 3 46

This case was one of wardship. So far as I can gather from the year Bk (which has not been translated) wardship was claimed for the Prince by virtue of the Manor of Berkhampstead which the king had granted to the Prince of Wales and his heirs kings of England.

It was held that the Prince of Wales had this prerogative on the ground that by the terms of the grant the Seignory was still annexed to the Crown and not be alienated.

[Note There is nothing to show that this refers to the Duchy of Cornwall]

At this point it is convenient to refer to the passage in Staunford relied on by the Duchy.

The passage is as follows—(sub tit Wardes) p11

Like law is it if the Kinge grant an honour to the Lord Prince and his heires Kings of England, it seemeth the better opinion in 21 Ed 3 fo 46 that the Lord Prince shall have therewith the King's prerogative because it is not severed from the Crowne after fourme as it is given, for none shall be inheritors therof but kinges of this Realm"

Staunford is there dealing with the question whether in granting away his Seignory the king can grant with the same his prerogative to the grantee.

It would seem that neither Fitzherbert nor Staunford are direct authorities for the broad proposition contended for the by the Duchy, but if the meaning in the case in the Year Book is correct it would seem to be applicable to any prerogative of the Crown.

1866 A.G. Pr of Wales v Crossman L.R. 1 Ex 381

The deft applied to change the venue and (at p 383) in argument the point is raised that the Crown not being named is not bound by statute nor by practice and therefore retains the same power which is also enjoyed by the Prince of Wales suing in subject of the royal possession of the Duchy.

Channell B deals with the argument at pp 386-7 but does not decide it though he says "We think that in this case the A.G. to the Prince of Wales must be taken to be in the same situation as A.G. to the Crown"

The application was dismissed on the grounds of balance of justice.

Prince of Wales other taxes

It appears that the Prince of Wales pays income tax, but does not pay rates. A bounty is given in lieu of rates.

The only ground upon which the Duchy can claim to escape rates would seem to be that these lands must be treated in the same was as Crown lands.

[For a discussion on the subject of the exemption of the Crown from charges in respect of land see Law Quarterly Oct 1912 p 378. There is nothing however in this article which is immediately germane to the present case]

1st Question

(i) Whether the contention of the Duchy of Cornwall that the Prince of Wales is not bound by the provisions of Acts of Parliament unless expressly named is correct.

I think that there is no need to cite authority for the proposition that the Crown is not bound by statute unless expressly named. The question would seem to be whether the Duchy is to be treated in the same way as the Crown.

I think that the question might be answered by saying that the Prince of Wales quâ Prince of Wales is bound by statute, but that quâ Duke of Cornwall and in respect of Duchy lands he is not bound.

The lands of the Duchy would appear to be in an anomalous position. They are not Crown lands strictly speaking, but they are analogous to Crown lands. Are one time they may be in the hands of the sovereign, at another time in those of the Prince. It would be difficult to hold that Acts of Parliament applied at one time and not at another. I think they must be treated as Crown Land.

2   *Whether it is the case that lands of the Duchy of Cornwall are not affected by the provisions of Acts imposing taxation unless express reference to or mention of these lands is made in any such Act*
   The answer to the above position covers this position.

3   *Whether the Prince of Wales is bound to make returns and to pay Minerals Rights Duty in respect of the rental value of rights granted by the Duchy of Cornwall to work minerals and of mineral way leaves and if so how these returns can be enforced and the Duty to be recovered.*

The instructions suggest that even though the Duchy may not be bound by statute, the mineral rights duty is not a tax on land and must therefore be paid by the Prince in his capacity of a subject.

I do not think that this is a tenable view. Mineral rights duty is imposed by sec 20 of the Finance (1909-1910) Act 1910 and is under Part I *which is headed Duties on Land Value. It is imposed upon the proprietor on the rent he actually receives or, if he works the minerals himself, upon a hypothetical rent. If it be correct to say that the statute does not apply to the Prince quâ Duke of Cornwall or to the Duchy lands I do not think that this tax can be due from him. The returns (s 20 ss (3)) are to be furnished by the proprietor and, quâ proprietor, the Prince is ex hypotheosi, not affected. Further the returns are in respect of rights to work minerals which are similarly not affected.*

(4) Whether during the minority of the Prince of Wales returns can be enforced and mineral rights duty be secured in respect of rights to work minerals and mineral way leaves granted by the Duchy.

Until the Duke of Cornwall is 21 his rights are to be exercised by the Sovereign or by any persons acting under the authority of the sovereign

26 & 27 Vic C 49 s 38[300]

Assuming that the Prince is liable, it would appear to be impossible to recover these duties while the Prince is under age inasmuch as it would appear to involve an information against the Crown.

(5) What course should be pursued by the Commissioners in order to compel the rendering of returns and the payment of sums due in respect of mineral rights duty which in the opinion of Counsel the Prince or the Duchy are bound to pay

It does not arise

I have not drafted an opinion as I see that Mr Finlay is with the LOO

---

300 Duchy of Cornwall Management Act 1863 section 38

BIBLIOGRAPHY

Manuscript Sources

British Library

Connock, R., *Account of the Duchy of Cornwall written for Henry Prince of Wales.* (1609)

Davies, Sir John, *Essay on the Rights of the Prince of Wales Relative to the Duchy of Cornwall.* (1613)

Crown Estate Files

Crown Estate File 64-00-11—Royal Mines

National Archives

AF 1/2159—Boundary Commission for England and Wales: European Parliamentary Elections Act 1978 (as amended). The Report by Mr. Assistant Commissioner G. D. Flather, Q.C. upon local enquiry held on 12/13 July 1988 on proposed Cornwall and Plymouth and Devon Parliamentary Constituencies.

Archon Code 1486—Duchy of Cornwall Office

BT 243/262—The Duchy of Cornwall: Legislation relating to right of wrecks of the sea (1856-1985)

C 197/18—Commission for management of the Duchy of Cornwall etc. (1827—1889)

CAB 129/51—Civil List (1952)

CRES 34/21—Wheal Newton Question between Crown and Duchy of Cornwall as to right to Royal Mines within duchy. (1859-1861).

CRES 34/49—Origin of Duchy of Cornwall rights to escheats in Dorchester (1921)

CRES 36/10—Hereditary revenues of the Crown, Civil List (1870)

CRES 37/49—Dartmouth and Torbay Railway Company claim of the Duchy of Cornwall. (1857-1865)

CRES 37/990—Cornwall Water of the Tamar Arbitration relating to the title between Crown and Duchy of Cornwall (1914-1938)

CRES 38/230—Crown Duchy of Cornwall Mines Under Foreshore and Seabed (1858)

CRES 58/694—Water of Tamar: arbitration between the Crown and the Duchy of Cornwall (1845—1889)

CRES 58/741—Seaward Limits between Crown and Duchy of Cornwall (1865—1870)

CUST 45/246—Memorandum on Taxation in Scilly Isles (1905)

IR 40/16546—Liability of Duchy of Cornwall to tax (1921)

IR 40/16549—Duchy of Cornwall—Law Officers Opinion (1921)

IR 40/16619—Liability of the Duchy of Cornwall to tax (1960-1962) (*closed*)

LCO 2/5136—Application of the revenues of the Duchy of Cornwall during minority of Duke of Cornwall also his next of kin (1952)

LO 3/467—Duchy of Cornwall—Land Tax and Valuation (1913)

LO 3/1177—Ecclesiastical Patronage of the Duchy of Cornwall (1937)

LRRO 11/15—Statements relating to the dispute between the crown and the Duchy of Cornwall concerning extent of seaward extent of Cornwall. (1865)

MT 9/5982—Duchy of Cornwall Investigations into manorial rights and title to unclaimed wreck (1868—1949)

MT 10/927—Board of Trade Correspondence and Papers (1904)

PREM 8/654—Research into Hereditary Revenues on provision of an establishment for Princess Elizabeth on her marriage (1947)

PREM 13/2906—Proposals for dealing with revenues of Duchy of Cornwall and proportion of which HRH Prince of Wales be asked to surrender (1969)

T 1/12673—Duchy of Cornwall—question of title to Royal Mines to be settled by arbitration (1880)

T 1/14831—Duchy of Cornwall title to gold and silver mines (1883)

T 1/16155—Arrangements for estate of late George IV to become property of Queen Victoria (1879)

T 1/16350—Duchy of Cornwall: Arbitration on Crown's right to royal gold and silver mines in Cornwall (1879)

T 38/837—Civil List Notes—The Welby Papers (1897)

T 160/284—Civil List—Report of the Committee appointed to examine the Civil List (1921)

T 160/632/1—Civil List; in relation to the hereditary and temporary revenues of the Crown (1936)

T 161/258—Amendments to Crown Lands Act (1925—1927)

T 168/52—Papers of Sir George Hamilton and Sir Edward Hamilton (1901-1904)

T 168/71—Papers relating to taxation and property rating of members of the Royal Family (1899-1904)

T 171/331—Select Committee on the Civil List (1936)

T 227/3380—Relationship between the Civil List and the hereditary revenues from Crown Estates and the Duchies of Cornwall and Lancaster (1962—1971)

TS 25/40—Duchy of Cornwall Accounts (1843)

TS 25/829—Whether fees payable to Queen's Remembrancer. (1865)

TS 25/1330—Treasure Trove—Luxulian Cornwall (1864)

TS 27/818—Treasure Trove: gold ornaments found at Amalevor Farm (1907—1932);

TS 45/5—Duchy Rights in the Water of the Tamar (1822—1880)

X355/48—Precept from Lord Warden of the Stannaries to Chief Constable (1821) (*Held at Cornwall Record Office*)

Public Hearing

House of Commons Public Accounts Committee—Report of Oral Evidence 7th February 2005.

Parliamentary Reports

House of Commons—Hereditary Revenues of the Crown during the reigns George III, George IV and William IV— Sir Robert Inglis, 1837 HC3 (London HMSO)

House of Commons—Report from the Select Committee appointed to inquire into the Accounts of Income and Expenditure of the Civil List January 1831 to 31 December 1836, 1837 HC22 (London HMSO)

House of Commons—Report from the Select Committee on Grants to Members of the Royal Family, 1889 HC271 (London HMSO)

House of Commons—Report from the Select Committee on the Civil List, 1901 HC 110 (London HMSO)

House of Commons—Report from the Select Committee on the Civil List, HC 211 (London HMSO) (1910)

House of Commons—Report from the Select Committee on the Civil List, 1935-36 HC74 (London HMSO)

House of Commons—Report from the Select Committee on the Civil List. 1971-72 HC 29 (London: HMSO)

Statutes in Force—10 Constitutional Law—Duchies of Cornwall and Lancaster. (1979)

House of Commons—Report of the Royal Trustees, 1993 HC464 (London HMSO)

House of Commons—Report of Political and Constitutional Reform Committee—The Impact of Queen's and Prince's

Consent on the Legislative Process 2014 HC 784 (London HMSO)

Other Reports

Thomas, J., Report to the Princes Council 21st February (1785).

The Tidal Estuaries, Foreshore and Under-Sea Minerals within and around The Coast of the County of Cornwall— Arbitration by Judge Sir John Patteson (1855 London Shaw & Co)

Duchy of Cornwall—Report to Her Majesty the Queen from the council of H.R.H. The Prince of Wales. (1862 London George E Eyre and William Spottiswoode)

Report of the Royal Commission on the Constitution. (The Kilbrandon Report) 1969-1973 Command 5460 (1973, London: HMSO)

Law Commission and HM Land Registry Land Registration for the 21st Century: A Conveyancing Revolution, Law Com No 271 (2001, London: HMSO)

Duchy of Cornwall Annual Report (2011)

Published Sources

Books

The Victoria History of the Counties of England—Cornwall (1906 London Victoria County Histories)

Angarrack, J., *Breaking the Chains.* (1999 Redruth Cornish Stannary Publications)

Angarrack, J., *Our Future is History.* (2002 Padstow Independent Academic Press)

Angarrack, J., *Scat t'Larrups?* (2008 Padstow Independent Academic Press)

Bainbridge, W., *A Treatise on the law of the Mines and Minerals.* (1856 London Butterworths)

Baring-Gould, S., *Cambridge County Geographies—Cornwall* (1910 Cambridge Cambridge University Press)

Barber, R., *Edward—Prince of Wales and Aquitaine*. (1978 Woodbridge The Boydell Press)

Barton, D. B., *A History of Tin Mining and Smelting in Cornwall*. (1967 Truro Bradford Barton)

Blackstone, Sir William, *Commentaries on the laws of England Volume 1*. (1832 London Collins and Hannay)

Bothwell, J., (editor) *The Age of Edward III*. (2001 Woodbridge Boydell and Brewer)

Brand, P., *The Origins of English Land Law: Milsom and After. The Making of the Common Law*. (1993 London Hambledon)

Brown, W., *The law of limitation as to real property including that of the crown and the Duke of Cornwall*. (1869 London H Sweet)

Buckley, J. A., *Medieval Cornish Stannary Charters 1201-1507*. (2001 Penryn Penhellick Publications)

Burnett, D., *A Royal Duchy—A Portrait of the Duchy of Cornwall*. (1996 Wimborne The Dovecote Press)

Carew, R., *The Survey of Cornwall*. (First published 1602) (2004 Exeter Devon and Cornwall Record Society)

Chitty, J., *Treatise on the Law of the Prerogatives of the Crown*. (1820 London Joseph Butterworth & Son)

Chynoweth, John, *Tudor Cornwall*. (2002 Stroud The History Press Ltd)

Cole, Dick., et al., *Mebyon Kernow & Cornish Nationalism*. (2003 Cardiff Welsh Academic Press)

Combellack, Dr Myrna, *The Camborne Play: A Verse Translation of Beunans Meriasek*. (1988 Redruth Dyllansow Truran)

Collier, R. P., *Treatise of the Law Relating to Mines*. (1855 London W G Benning & Co.)

Concanen, G., *A Report of the Trial at Bar Rowe v Brenton*. (1830 London Salmon and Cunningham)

Cornwall, J., *Revolt of the Peasantry 1549*. (1977 London Routledge & Kegan Paul Ltd.)

Cooper, J.P.D., *Propaganda and the Tudor State* (2003 Oxford Clarendon Press)

Deacon, B., *Cornwall—A Concise History*. (2007 Cardiff University of Wales Press)

Denholm-Young, N., *Seigniorial Administration in England*. (1937 Oxford Oxford University Press)

Denholm-Young, N., *Richard of Cornwall*. (1947 Oxford Basil Blackwell)

Dodridge, Sir John., *An Historical Account of the Ancient and Modern State of the Principality of Wales, Dutchy of Cornwall and Earldom of Chester*. (written in 1630 published 1714 London J Roberts)

Duffin, A., *Faction and faith: politics and religion of the Cornish gentry before the Civil War*. (1996 Exeter University of Exeter Press)

Elliott-Binns, L. E., *Medieval Cornwall*. (1955 London Methuen & Co Ltd.)

Erskine May Parliamentary Practice 24th Edition (2004 London LexisNexis)

Fraser, R., *General View of the County of Cornwall*. (1794 London Macrae)

Gill, C., (Ed.) *The Duchy of Cornwall*. (1987 Newton Abbot David & Charles).

Green, G. K., et al., *Douglas & Green on the Law of harbours, coast and pilotage*. (1997 London, LLP.)

Haines, J., *Case between Sir William Clayton, Bart, and the Duchy of Cornwall*. (1834 London, J Betts.)

Haines, J., *The history of the constitution of the Duchy of Cornwall and its tenants*. (1834 London, J. Betts.)

Hale, Sir Matthew, *The Prerogatives of the King*. (1976 (Written 1640—1676) Cambridge Mass. Selden Society)

Hall, P., *Royal Fortune, Tax, Money and the Monarchy*. (1992 London, Bloomsbury)

Halliday, F. E., *A History of Cornwall*, (1959 Thirsk House of Stratus.)

Halsbury's Laws of England. 12(1) (2010 London LexisNexis)

Harrison, Sir George., *A Report of the Laws and Jurisdiction of the Stannaries.* (1835 London Longman Rees Orme Brown Green and Longman)

Harrison, Sir George, *Memoir respecting the Hereditary Revenues of the Crown and the Revenues of the Duchies of Cornwall and Lancaster.* (1838 London)

Hatcher, J., *Rural Economy and Society in the Duchy of Cornwall 1300-1500.* (1970 Cambridge Cambridge University Press.)

Heath, R., *A Natural and Historical Account of the Islands of Scilly.* (1750 London R Manby & H S Cox)

Henderson, C., *Essays in Cornish History.* (1935 Truro D Bradford Barton)

Hitchins, F., and Drew, S., *The History of Cornwall.* (1824 Helston W Penaluna)

Hoyle, R. W., (Ed.) *The Estates of the English Crown 1558-1640.* (2002 Cambridge Cambridge University Press)

Hudson, J., *Land Law and Lordship in Anglo Norman England.* (1994 Stroud Clarendon Press)

Hull, P. L., *The Caption of Seisin of the Duchy of Cornwall (1337).* (1971 Exeter Devon and Cornwall Record Society)

Ing, N. D., *Bona Vacantia.* (1971 London, Butterworths)

Jack, Sir Malcolm, (Ed.) *Erskine May—Parliamentary Practice 24th Edition* (2011 London LexisNexis)

Jenkin, A. K. H., *The Story of Cornwall.* (1945 London J M Dent)

Jenner, H., *A Handbook of the Cornish Language.* (1904 London David Nutt; 2010 Cathair na Mart: Evertype)

Kirkhope, J. *This Miniature Nation.* (2014 Amazon eBooks)

Kowaleski, M., *The Havener's Accounts of the Earldom and Duchy of Cornwall 1287-1356.* (2001 Exeter Devon and Cornwall Record Society)

Laity, P., Saunders, T., Kent, A.M., *The Reason Why—Cornwall's Status in Constitutional and International Law* (2001 Bro Kernow)

BIBLIOGRAPHY

Lewis, G. R., *The Stannaries: A Study of the Medieval Tin Miners of Cornwall and Devon.* (1965 Truro D Barton Bradford)

Lyon, A., *Constitutional History of the United Kingdom.* (2002 London, Cavendish Publishing Ltd)

Lyson, S., *History of Topography of Cornwall.* (1814 London Cadell & Greenland)

Manning, J., *Report of Cases argued and determined in the Court of Kings Bench.* (1830 London S Sweet)

Matthews, G. F., *The Isles of Scilly.* (1960 London George Ronald)

Midgley, L. Margaret, (ed.) *Ministers' Accounts of the Earldom of Cornwall 1296 1297.* (1942 London Camden Third Series)

Moore, G., *Essay on the Rights of the Prince of Wales relative to the Dutchy of Cornwall.* (1795 London)

Moore, S., *A History of the Foreshore and the law relating thereto.* (1888 London Stevens and Haynes)

Morris, W. A., *The medieval English sheriff 1300.* (1927 Manchester Manchester University Press)

Mortimer, I., *The Perfect King—The Life of Edward III—Father of the English Nation.* (2006 London Jonathan Cape)

Mortimer, I., *Medieval Intrigue.* (2010 London Continuum International Publishing Group)

Murley, C., et al (eds) *Cornwall: One of the Four Nations of Britain.* (1996 Redruth)

Mustill, J. P., *Summer needs no brightening—An gof and the 1497 Cornish Rebellion.* (1997 Penzance Blue Elvan Press)

Norden, J., *A topographic Historic Description of Cornwall.* (1728 London Christopher Bateman)

Payton, P., *The Making of Modern Cornwall.* (1992 Redruth Dyllansow Truran)

Payton, P., *A Vision of Cornwall—Duchy Originals.* (2002 Fowey Alexander Associates)

Payton, P., *Cornwall—A History.* (2004 Fowey Cornwall Editions Limited)

Pearce, T., *The Laws and Customs of the Stannaries in the Counties of Cornwall and Devon.* (1725 London D Browne)

Pearse, R., *The Land Beside the Celtic Sea—Aspects of Cornwall Past.* (1983 Redruth Truran)

Pennington, R. R., *Stannary Law.* (1973 Newton Abbot David & Charles)

Peto, Sir S Morton, *Taxation, Its Levy and Expenditure, Past and Future; being an enquiry into our financial policy.* (1866 New York D Appleton & Co.)

Picken, W. M. M., *A Medieval Cornish Miscellany.* (2000 Chichester Phillimore & Co Ltd)

Pitt, T., *The State of Proceedings of the Convocation or Parliament for the Stannaries of the County of Cornwall.* (1751 London R Baldwin).

Polwhele, R., *History of Cornwall.* (1816 Truro Law and Whittaker)

Pycroft, J. W., *Arena Cornubiae: or the claims of the commissioners of woods and forests to the sea coast and banks of tidal rivers in Cornwall and Devon.* (1856 London W G Benning & Co)

Rogers, A., *The law relating to mines, minerals and quarries in Great Britain and Ireland including the rights of the crown, the duchy of cornwall and local laws and customes.* (1876 London Stevens Sons and Haynes)

Rowe, D. J., *Cornwall and the Age of the Industrial Revolution.* (1953 Liverpool Liverpool University Press)

Rowse, A.L., *Tudor Cornwall.* (1941 London Macmillan)

Rowse, A. L., *West Country Stories.* (1945 London Macmillan)

Rowse, A. L., *The Little Land of Cornwall.* (1986 Stroud Alan Sutton Publishing)

Smirke, Sir Edward, *Case of Vice against Thomas with an Appendix of Records and Documents on the early History of the Tin Mines in Cornwall.* (1843 London Saunders and Benning)

Soulsby, I., *A History of Cornwall.* (1986 Chichester Phillimore)

Staunford, Sir William, *The Pleas of the Crown*. (1560 London Tottel)

Stoyle, M., *West Britons—Cornish Identities and the Early Modern British State*. (2002 Exeter University of Exeter Press)

Sunkin, M., Payne, S., (ed.) *The Nature of the Crown*. (1999 Oxford Oxford University)

Thorne, Caroline and Frank, (eds) *Domesday Book—Cornwall*. (1979 Chichester Phillimore)

Tonkin, T., *A Journal of the Convocation of four and Twenty Stannators*. (1710 Truro Royal Institute of Cornwall)

Tout, T. F., *The Political History of England 1216-1377*. (1905 London Longmans Green & Co.)

Tout, T.F., (ed.) *Chapters in the Administrative History of Medieval England*. (1930 Manchester Manchester University Press.)

Tregonning, J., *The Laws of the Stannaries of Cornwall with Marginal Notes*. (1808 Truro J. Tregonning)

Trembath, B., *Perranporth and Perranzabuloe Parish*. (1992 Truro Lodenek Press.)

Trevithick Society *Laws of the Stannaries of Cornwall Made at the Convocation or Parliament of Tinners*. (1974 Penzance The Trevithick Society)

Tuck, A., *Crown and Nobility 1272-1461*. (1985 Oxford Blackwell)

Watkins, C., *An inquiry into the title and powers of His Majesty, as guardian of the Duchy of Cornwall, during the late minority of its Duke*. (1795 London, Gale Ecco.)

Whetter, J., *Cornwall in the 13th Century*, (1998 Gorran Lyfrow Trelyspen.)

Whetter, J., *Cornwall in the seventeenth Century*. (1978 Padstow Lodenek Press)

Whetter, J., *Cornish people in the fifteenth century*. (1999 Gorran Lyfrow Trelyspen)

Yates, J. B., *The Rights and Jurisdictions of the County Palatine of Chester etc.* (1856 Manchester The Chetham Society.)

Journal Articles

Alexander, J.J., "The Devon-Cornwall Boundary" (1928—1929) *Devon and Cornwall Notes and Queries* Volume XV pp 271—274

Alexander, J.J., "Escheators of Devon 1300-1450" (1934-35) *Devon and Cornwall Notes and Queries* Volume 18 pp 164—168

Bartlett, R.T. "Taxation and the Royal Family—I." (1983) *British Tax Review* No 2 pp 99—112

Bartlett, R.T. "Taxation and the Royal Family—II." (1983) *British Tax Review* No 3 pp 138—157

Brazier, R., "The constitutional position of the Prince of Wales." (1995) *Public Law.* pp 401-416

Brazier, R., "Legislating about the monarchy." (2007) *Cambridge Law Review* pp 294-309

Clowes, R L., "Escheators of Devon and Cornwall." (1930-31) *Devon and Cornwall Notes and Queries* XVI: pp 201-202

Coates, Mary., "The Duchy of Cornwall: Its History and Administration 1640 to 1660." (1927) *Transactions of the Royal Historical Society*: pp 135-169

Cruickshanks, E., "The Convocation of the Stannaries of Cornwall: The Parliament of Tinners 1703-1752." (1986) *Parliaments, Estates and Representation* Volume 6 Part 1. pp 59-67

Deacon, B., "Review Article—Breaking the Chains and Forging New Links" (2000) *Cornish Studies—Journal of the Institute of Cornish Studies* Volume 8 pp 231-234

Deacon, B., "Review Article—Propaganda and the Tudor State or Propaganda of the Tudor Historians" (2003) *Cornish Studies—Journal of the Institute of Cornish Studies* Volume 11 pp 317-328

Evans, D. L., "Some Notes on the Principality of Wales in the Time of the Black Prince (1343-1376)." (1925-26) *The Transactions of the Honourable Society of Cymmrodorion* Session pp 25—101

Gray, A., "Immunity of the Crown from Statute and Suit." (2010) *Canberra Law Review* 1 pp 1-35

Haslam, G., "The Duchy and Parliamentary Representation 1547-1640." (1980) *Journal of the Royal Institute of Cornwall* viii(iii): pp 224- 242

Hatcher, J. "Myths, Miners and Agricultural Communities." (1974) *The Agricultural History Review.* Vol. 22 Part 1 pp 54-61

Hatcher, J., "A Diversified Economy: Later Medieval Cornwall." (1969) *Economic History Review* 2nd series xxii no 2. pp 208-227

Hatcher, J., "Non-Manorialism in Medieval Cornwall." (1970) *The Agricultural History Review* 18. pp 1—16

Hull, P. L., "Richard Carew's Discourse on the Duchy Suit 1594." (1962) *Journal of the Royal Institute of Cornwall* iv(ii): pp 181-251.

Jenner, H., "Cornwall a Celtic Nation." (1905) *Celtic Review*: pp 234-246

Karraker, C. H., "Royal Fish." (1936) *Quarterly Review* 267: pp 129-136.

Kuhn, W., "Queen Victoria's Civil List: What did she do with it?" (1993) *The Historical Journal* Volume 36 No 3. 645-665

Pearce-Crump, D., "Royal Taxation." (1994) *British Tax Review* pp 635-646

Peter, O., "A Tabular Statement of the Earls and Dukes of Cornwall from AD 1068 to A.D. 1914." (1915) *Journal of the Royal Institute of Cornwall Volume* XX. pp 107—115

Percival, G., "The Civil List and the Hereditary Revenues of the Crown." (1901) *Fortnightly Review* March pp 1-11

Reitan, E. A., "The Civil List in the Eighteenth Century Politics: Parliamentary Supremacy versus the Independence of the Crown." (1996) *The Historical Journal* 9(3): 318-337.

Rowse, A. L., "Review of 'The Duchy of Cornwall'." (1990) *The English Historical Review* 105(416): p 721.

Salzman, L. F., "Mines and Stannaries." (1950) *English Government at Work* pp 67-104

Stansfield, R.E., "A Duchy Officer and a gentleman: The career connections of Avery Cornburgh (d.1487)." (2011) *Cornish Studies* 19 pp 9—34

Stoyle, M., "Pagans or Paragons? Images of the Cornish during the English Civil War." (1996) *English Historical Review* Volume 111 No 441. pp 299-323

Stoyle, M., "The Dissidence of Despair: Rebellion and Identity in Early Modern Cornwall." (1999) *Journal of British Studies* Volume 38 No 4.pp 423-444

Tait, J. "The First Earl of Cornwall." (1929) *English Historical Review* Volume 44 No 173. p 86

Youings, J.A., "The Council of the West" (1960) *Transactions of the Royal Historical Society* 5th Series Part No. X pp 41—59

Pamphlets

Cowethas Flamank, *The Detectable County—Special Report Number 6.*(1986)

Green, R., *What is the Duchy of Cornwall.* (1985 Redruth Cornwall Branch Communist Party of Great Britain)

The Stannary Parliament, *The Constitution of Cornwall or Kernow—The County of the West Britons.* (1993 Redruth Cornish Stannary Parliament)

Unpublished Theses

Chynoweth, J., *The gentry of Tudor Cornwall.* (1994) Thesis (Ph.D.) University of Exeter

Cullum, D. H., *Society and Economy in West Cornwall 1588-1750.* (1994) Thesis (Ph.D.) University of Exeter.

Duffin, A., *The Political Allegiances of the Cornish Gentry 1600-1642.* (1989) Thesis (Ph.D.) University of Exeter

Haslam, G., *An Administrative Study of the Duchy of Cornwall 1500 to 1650.* (1975) Thesis (Ph.D.) Louisiana State University

Page, M., *Royal and comital government and the local community in thirteenth-century Cornwall.* (1995) Thesis (Ph.D.) University of Oxford

Payton, P., *Modern Cornwall: changing nature of periphery.* (1989) Thesis (Ph.D.) University of Plymouth.

Speight, H. M., *Local government and politics in Devon and Cornwall 1509-1549, with special reference to the South-Western Rebellion.* (1991) Thesis (Ph.D.) University of Sussex.

Tyldesley, C. J., *The Crown and the Local Communities in Devon and Cornwall from 1377 to 1422.* (1978) Thesis (Ph.D.) University of Exeter.

Whiting, R., *The Reformation in the South West of England.* (1977) Thesis (Ph.D.) University of Exeter.

Williams, R., *County and municipal government in Cornwall, Devon, Dorset and Somerset 1649-1660.* (1981) Thesis (Ph.D.) University of Bristol.

List of Statutes

Administration of Estates Act 1925
Bill of Rights 1688
Civil List Act 1697
Civil List Act 1760
Civil List Act 1837
Civil List Act 1901
Civil List Act 1910
Civil List Act 1936
Civil List Act 1952
Civil List Act 1972
Coinage Abolition Act 1838
Companies Act 1985
Companies Act 2006
Constitutional Reform Act 2005
Constitutional Reform and Governance Act 2010
Convocation Act (Cornwall) 1588
Cornwall Submarine Mines Act 1858
Crown Private Estate Act 1800
Crown Private Estates Acts 1862 and 1873
Crown Proceedings Act 1947
Crown Suits Act 1769 (nullum tempus act)

Dangerous Vessels Act 1985
Dangerous Substances in Harbour Areas Regulations 1987
De Prærogativa Regis 1324
Duchies of Lancaster and Cornwall (Accounts) Act 1838
Duchy of Cornwall Act 1812
Duchy of Cornwall Act 1844
Duchy of Cornwall (No 2) Act 1844
Duchy of Cornwall (limitation of actions. etc) Act 1860
Duchy of Cornwall Lands Act 1862
Duke of Cornwall Leases etc Act 1842
Duchy of Cornwall Management Act 1863
Duchy of Cornwall Management Act 1868
Duchy of Cornwall Management Act 1893
Duchy of Cornwall Management Act 1982
Environmental Information Regulations 2004

Escheators Act 1509

Exchequer Court Act 1842

Finance (1909-1910) Act 1910

Great Charter of Creation of the Duchy of Cornwall, 17 March 1337

Harbours Act 1964

House of Lords Act 1999

Inclosure Act 1845

Judicature Act 1873

Land Tax Act 1798

Leasehold Reform Act 1967

Leasehold Reform, Housing and Urban Development Act 1993

Limitation Act 1980

Merchant Shipping Act 1854

Merchant Shipping Act 1995

Merchant Shipping and Maritime Security Act 1977

Miscellaneous Financial Provisions Act 1983

Pier and Harbour Order Confirmation (No. 4) Act 1890

Pilotage Act 1987

Prevention of Pollution (Reception Facilities) Order 1984

Privilege of Parliament Act 1512

Reserved Forces Act 1996

Royal Mines Act 1688

Royal Mines Act 1693

Settled Land Act 1925

Sovereign Grant Act 2011

St. Mary's (Isles of Scilly) Harbour Revision Order 2007

Stamp Act 1891

Stannaries Act 1641

Stannaries Act 1836

Stannary Act 1855

Stannary Courts (Abolition) Act 1896

Taxation Act 1702

Tenure Abolition Act 1660

Tin Duties Act 1838

Treasure Act 1996

Quo Warranto Act 1290

Wildlife and Countryside Act 1981

List of Cases

Alcock v Cooke (1829) (5 Bing 340)

Attorney General v Ceely (1660) (Wight 208)

Attorney General v HRH Prince Ernest Augustus of Hanover (1957) (1957 W L R 1) (1957 A.C. 436)

Attorney General of the Duchy of Lancaster v Duke of Devonshire (1884) (14 QBD 195)

Attorney General to the Prince of Wales v Crossman (1866) (L.R. 1 Ex 381)

Attorney General to the Prince of Wales v The Bristol Waterworks Company (1855) (156 E.R. 699) (10 Ex. 884)

Attorney General to H.R.H. Prince of Wales, Duke of Cornwall v The Mayor and Commonalty of the Borough of Plymouth (1754) (Wight 134)

Attorney General to H.R.H., Prince of Wales, Duke of Cornwall v Sir John St. Aubyn and others (1811) (Wight 167)

Attorney General to the Isle of Man v Cowley and Kinrade (1859) (12 Moore PCC 2)

Boscawen v Chaplin (1536) (Harleian Manuscripts 6380 fol. 9)

Cabinet Office v Information Commissioner (2012) (EA/2012)0200)

Case of Mines (1567) (1 Plowd 310 at 315-316)

Chasyn v Lord Stourton (1553) (1 Dyer 94a) (73 E.R. 205)

Department of Business Innovation & Skill v The Information Commissioner (2012) (EA/2012/0057)

Devon Peerage Case (1831) (5 Bli NS 220) (2 Dow & Cl 200) (2 State Tr NS 659)

Duchy of Cornwall Case (1613) (1 Ves Sen 292)

Duchy of Lancaster Case (1561) (1 Plowd 212)

Dyke v Walford (1846) 5 Moo PCCC 434

Evans v Information Commissioner and Others (2012) UKUT 313 (AAC))

Frederick Richard Albert Trull v Restormel Borough Council (1994) (1994 WL 1062112)

The Guelder Rose (1927) (136 LT 226)

Hensloe's Case (1599) (9 Coke Reports 36b)

Jewison v Dyson (1842) (9 Meeson and Welsby 540) (152 E.R. 228)

The Kings Case (1604) (7 Co Rep 32a)

Kirkhope v Information Commission and The National Archive (2012) (EA/2011/0185)

Langworth v Scott (1616) (3 Bulstr 183)

Lomax v Holmden (1749) (1 Vesey Senior 290) (27 E.R. 1038)

Lopez v Andrew (1826) (3 Man & Ry K.B. 329n)

Manchester Corporation v Manchester Palace of Varieties Ltd (1955) (2 WLR 440) (1 All ER 387)

Mercer v Denne (1902) (M 417 (1905) 2 Ch 538)

Mersey Docks v Cameron (1865) (11 H.L.C. 443)

Michael Bruton v ICO and The Duchy of Cornwall (2011) (EA/2010/0182)

Pearce v Grundy (1818) (Decided by Vice Warden of the Stannaries 7 April 1818)

Penryn Corporation v Holm (1877) (2 Ex D 328) (46 LJQB 506) (25 WR 498) (37 LT 133)

Prince Henry's Charter Case (1611) (1 Bulst 133)

The Princes Case (1606) (8 Rep 1a) (77 E.R. 481)

R v Cook (1790) (3 T.R. 519)

R v East Powder Magistrates' Court Ex Parte Lampshire (1979) (2 All ER 329)

R v Inhabitants of Hermitage (1692) (Carth. 239) (90 ER 743)

Re: Oriental Bank (1884) (L.R. 28 C.D. 643)

Re: Salisbury Railway and Market House Co (1967) (3 WLR 651)

Resolution of the Judges 1608

Resolution of the Privy Council 1632

Regina v Ernest Nute and Others (2001) (Case No T20010073)

Rex v Mayor and Jurats of Hastings (1882) (1 Dowl & Ry. 148)

Rex v Steward of Havering (1822) (2 Dowl. & Ry 176n)

Rex v Wells Corporation (1836) (4 Dowl. 562)

Rowe v Brenton (1828) (8 B & C 737) (3 Man & Ry KB 133) (108 E.R. 1217) (Concanen's Rep 1)

Re Salisbury Railway and Market House Co. (1967) (3 WLR 651)

Sheriff (1704) (3 Salkeld 322 91 E.R. 849)

Sir Henry Constables Case (1601) (5 Co Rep 106a)

Smartsource Drainage & Water Reports Ltd v ICO (2011) (1 Info LR 1498)

Strode's Case (1512) (1 Hats. 85) (Howell's State Trials 294)

The Solicitor to the Duchy of Cornwall v Canning (1880) (5 P.D. 114 Probate)

Sturla v Feccia (1880) (5 App. Cas 623, 643)

Three Rivers District Council and others v Governor and Company of the Bank of England (2004) (UKHL 48)

Tregilgas v Dingey (1843)

Re: *Treverbyn Trevanion Clay Works (1872)* (Reported in Royal Institute of Cornwall Gazette 1 June 1972)

Trewynard v Killigrew (1562) (4 and 7 Elizabeth 1)

Trewynnard v Roscarrack (1564) (4 Coke's Institutes 229)

Weymouth v Nugent (1865) (6 B & S 22)

Wilkes Peerage Claim (1869) (LR 4 HL 126)

Willion v Berkley (1561) (1 Plowden 223) (75 E.R. 339) (KB)

About the Author

John Kirkhope has been awarded degrees and post-graduate qualifications from the Open University, Nottingham Trent University, Bristol University, and Cambridge. He was recently awarded a Doctorate in Philosophy from Plymouth University; his thesis was an examination of the Duchy of Cornwall and is entitled *The Duchy of Cornwall—A Feudal Remnant*. Professionally John qualified as a solicitor and a Notary Public. The law and its arcane and dusty corners have been of interest of him for many years.

Members of Parliament and Members of the House of Lords consult John on matters relating to the Laws of Cornwall and the Duchy of Cornwall. His advice has also been sought by the Devon and Cornwall Police. Recently John was asked to submit evidence to two House of Commons Select Committees.

John has been interviewed for the Today Programme on Radio 4, Radio Devon and has made appearances on two BBC Television programmes.

Lightning Source UK Ltd.
Milton Keynes UK
UKOW03f1429090614

233099UK00001B/16/P